When the Crowd Didn't Roar

T0059993

KEVIN COWHERD

WHEN THE CROWD DIDN'T ROAR

How Baseball's Strangest Game Ever
GAVE A BROKEN CITY HOPE

University of Nebraska Press

LINCOLN & LONDON

To my wife and best friend always, Nancy. To my wonderful son, Sean, and his family: Karlye, Madeline, and Jack. To my beautiful daughter, Chrissie, and terrific son, Jamie.

To the best mom in the world, the incomparable Noreen Cowherd. And to my great friend Rob Hiaasen, too soon gone from this earth.

Go placidly amid the noise and haste, and remember what peace there may be in silence.

MAX EHRMANN, "Desiderata"

Acknowledgments

A PROJECT OF THIS nature could never be completed without the help of many others, and I am indebted to all who assisted.

None of it would have been possible without the tremendous cooperation of the Baltimore Orioles. I would especially like to thank Executive Vice President John Angelos, Vice President of Communications and Marketing Greg Bader, and Director of Public Relations Kristen Hudak for the access they provided, their tireless help in lining up interviews, and their insights into the team's operations during the five tumultuous days that form the setting for most of this book.

(A quick thanks, too, to Coordinator of Public Relations Kailey Adams, tasked with the all-important mission of making sure I was on the Orioles' parking list and thereby able to avoid the usurious rates at downtown garages.)

Manager Buck Showalter and Orioles players Zach Britton, Chris Davis, Ubaldo Jimenez, Adam Jones, and Caleb Joseph were unfailingly generous with their time and candid in their recollections of what it was like to play behind locked gates, in an empty stadium, during baseball's strangest game ever. My heartfelt thanks to all of them.

So willing and eager was he to recount the events of that day that Chris Davis spent much of an evening with me at a bakery in suburban Baltimore and wouldn't let me buy him anything more than a coffee. Or maybe it was an orange juice. Adam Jones graciously invited me into his home and with his father-in-law, attorney and former NFL tight end Jean Fugett, listening in attentively, provided much-needed perspective on the angry youths rising up in Baltimore's poorest neighborhoods and the not-so-subtle racial bias so many African American ballplayers—even those who are fabulously wealthy—face to this day.

A special thanks, also, to Lt. Dennis Reinhard, the Baltimore Police Department commander at Camden Yards, who with infinite patience and minimum use of police jargon and acronyms walked me through the security procedures that kept so many fans safe when the protests over Freddie Gray's death first turned violent. My thanks also to Vernon Conaway Jr., the Maryland Stadium Authority's vice president of public safety and security, who diligently schooled me on the role that the ballpark's emergency operations center played that day.

Kweisi Mfume, the civil rights activist, former Maryland congressman, and former NAACP president, deserves special thanks for his invaluable insights into Baltimore's devastating 1968 riots following the assassination of Martin Luther King and for his keen analysis of how little has changed, on a socioeconomic level, for the city's downtrodden.

A note of thanks, too, to the administrative folks at Woodlawn Cemetery and Chapel for their help on my visits to the final resting place of Freddie Gray.

Others who offered their cheerful assistance, extensive knowledge, and memories of both the April 2015 unrest that gripped Baltimore and the historic "No-Fans Game" include Joe Angel, Mel Antonen, Jonathan Bernhardt, Jerry Coleman, Dan Connolly, Bob Davidson, Paul Doren, Rich Dubroff, Dan Duquette, Eduardo Encina, Pete Gilbert, Craig Heist, Kendall Hilton, Brett Hollander, Jim Hunter, Brad Hutcheson, Lee Igel, Mark Jacobsen, Colleen Kane, Roch Kubatko, Steve Melewski, Dawn Merguerian, Jim Palmer, Sharon Reuter, Chris Riehl, Dan Rodricks, Bill Rose, Rick Rutherford, Peter Schmuck, Brandon Scott, Bill Stetka, Gary Thorne, Mark Viviano, Hunter Wendelstedt, and Bernard C. "Jack" Young. I will never be able to repay your kindness.

Thanks to my buddy Kevin Richardson, ace videographer and photographer and former colleague at the *Baltimore*

Sun, for his invaluable help and advice in selecting photos for this book.

A special thanks to my agent, Janet Pawson, for believing in this project—a sort of non-baseball baseball book—from the very beginning. And to Rob Taylor, my patient and able editor at the University of Nebraska Press, who also recognized the unique nature of this story and who provided steadfast support and guidance over these many months.

Finally a special thanks to John Eisenberg: friend, former *Sun* colleague, and gracious mentor to so many aspiring authors in the Baltimore area and beyond. John encouraged me from the start, quieted my doubts, and offered wise counsel about the publishing world when I wondered if this book would ever see the light of day.

And now it has.

Prologue

ADAM JONES AWAKENS FROM a fitful sleep and gazes at the alarm clock.

Damn! Almost 7:30 already . . .

From the other room he can hear his thirteen-month-old son, August, stirring. This is Jones's morning routine as a new dad: Drag himself out of bed in the early hours of a spring morning. Shuffle bleary-eyed to the little man's crib before he goes into full meltdown mode. Bring him to his mama, Audie, who's still sleeping peacefully.

Let her work her magic.

Yet even as the Baltimore Orioles' All-Star center fielder throws off the covers, the worry that's gnawed at him for days returns.

What's going to happen to this city? he wonders.

He flashes back to when he was a little kid, seven years old, a black man named Rodney King arrested and beaten by white cops in Los Angeles, the whole thing captured on videotape. Then came a trial, a stunning acquittal, and folks pouring into the streets of South Central to vent their rage, beating people and burning buildings for days and days.

Is that going to happen here?

It's a fair question right now. And Adam Jones is by no means the only one asking it.

Two days earlier Baltimore had exploded in a frightening spate of rioting following the death of a twenty-five-year-old African American named Freddie Gray from injuries suffered in police custody. Images of the looting and burning had been flashed all over the country—all over the world, for that matter—as Baltimore joined Ferguson, Missouri; Staten Island, New York; Cleveland; and North Charleston, South Carolina, as a place of angry demonstrations following fatal encounters between young black men and law enforcement officials.

Yet now, less than thirty-six hours after the worst of the turmoil, with thousands of National Guard troops patrolling the streets to keep the uneasy peace, the Orioles are about to play the Chicago White Sox at Camden Yards in what Jones knows will be the strangest baseball game of his life.

Not only is the city still reeling, but, with dozens of police officers normally assigned to the stadium needed elsewhere to maintain order, the game will be held behind locked gates—the only one ever played without fans since the Major Leagues started in 1869.

Some way to make history, he thinks ruefully.

Even as he sips his morning coffee and pulls on his black Jordan sweats, long-sleeved Nike shirt, black camouflage hoodie, and camo FBI cap—"my game-day ensemble" he calls it—he can't stop fixating on how bizarre it all sounds.

We're playing a game that actually counts in the standings . . .
In front of absolutely no one . . .
In a town that could explode again at any moment . . .
Man, this is gonna be so freakin' weird.

By eleven he's climbing into his truck, a Ford F-150 Raptor with a sick matte-black paint job, tinted windows, and a bone-rattling sound system. A total stealth look, he calls it. It's a fitting set of wheels for a young superstar athlete, especially one in the midst of a six-year, $85.5 million contract extension that's the richest in team history.

Adam Jones loves his truck. It's a proud symbol of his grit and perseverance, a shiny reminder of just how far he's come.

During his senior year of high school his dad had given him an '88 Porsche with a Volvo engine. No one had ever heard of such a thing. Being busy with school and sports, Adam didn't get to drive it much. Which was just as well, since the car ran pretty much the way you'd expect a Porsche with a Volvo engine to run.

His sister borrowed it once, called him back three days later. Got right down to business: "Uh, yeah, the car won't start."

Adam doesn't have problems like that with his cars anymore. Audie, on the other hand, hates the Raptor. She especially hates the unearthly roar it makes when Adam turns the key in the ignition. That's when she'll jab a finger in his direction and hiss: "Do you *have* to make all that noise? The baby's sleeping!"

Adam has to laugh when that happens. She's right, of course. The damn truck could wake up babies in Guam, never mind one snoozing peacefully under his own roof.

The drive to the ballpark, which normally takes twenty-five minutes, is quicker today. There's far less traffic than usual on the main arteries headed into town. It's Wednesday, April 29, 2015, a gorgeous spring morning, sunny and warm, perfect conditions for today's 2:05 p.m. start.

Normally on his way to the ballpark Jones would be mentally preparing himself for the pitcher he's about to face. Today it's Chicago right-hander Jeff Samardzija, who stands six feet five inches, has a fastball that touches ninety-eight on the radar gun, and is wild enough to make your feet sweat when you step in against him.

But Jones, the American League's leading hitter this young season, hasn't given the big guy a single thought.

Instead what he's focused on is this: with the national media in town to cover the unrest—and with nearly a hundred reporters expected on hand for this unprecedented game—he's asked the Orioles if he could say a few words at a pregame news conference.

As the face of the franchise and the city's most-celebrated African American athlete, he feels an obligation to talk about the civic eruption, to explain why so many in this majority-black city reached their breaking point, to try to put it in perspective for those who already think of Baltimore as nothing more than a dangerous, drug-infested backwater between Philadelphia and Washington DC.

Only one problem, Jones thinks now. *What exactly am I*

gonna say? What am I gonna say so Mama doesn't call me and go: "Son, what the HELL *did you just say?"*

A few minutes into the ride he calls his older brother, Anson Wright, in California. The two have always been close. Jones can talk to Anson about anything. Maybe he's got some advice on how to handle this.

But for one of the few times in his life Anson has nothing for him. No words of encouragement. No pointers on what to say.

Nada.

Instead, after Jones tells him what he's about to do in front of a roomful of mostly white, middle-aged media types, with this fierce unraveling of the city very much on everyone's mind, Anson makes this fluttery sound with his lips.

Like: Oh, man, good luck with that . . .

Wow, Jones thinks, *he's dumbfounded! He's damn speechless!*

Moments later, as Jones takes the Maryland Avenue exit off I-83 and makes his way to Lombard Street, the enormity of the riot's impact becomes apparent.

An eerie stillness blankets the city. The sidewalks are mostly deserted. A sickly odor of charred buildings and burned-out cars, borne on a light coating of ash, hangs in the air. The faint wail of sirens can be heard in the distance.

Police and news helicopters clatter across the skies. Hundreds of National Guard troops wielding automatic weapons line the downtown thoroughfares of Pratt and Lombard.

Jones is used to seeing soldiers in uniform on the streets of his hometown of San Diego, with its sprawling military bases. But not here in Baltimore. And as he saw from news reports on TV last night, these troops, with their riot helmets and tactical vests and tense expressions, appear to be in full battle mode.

They seem more than willing to kick some ass if anything goes off.

Unbelievable, Jones thinks. *We're playing ball in the middle of this?*

Off to his left, not far away, there's another jarring sight: the tourist mecca of the Inner Harbor, devoid of the usual crowds of latte-sipping office workers and vacationing moms and dads pushing baby strollers that the warm weather brings. The same Inner Harbor, with its glittering shops, bars and restaurants, that African American leaders have pointed to for years to illustrate the inequality between Baltimore's have and have-not neighborhoods.

On the network and cable news shows over the past few days, breathless commentaries about the turmoil in the streets invariably end with one talking head or another asking incredulously: "How did it ever get this bad?"

Jones has to shake his head whenever he hears that.

How did it get this bad? Oh, that one's easy. He can give them chapter and verse about all the things that went wrong.

Sure, he has the big house in the suburbs now, with the nice pool, three cars in the driveway and all the requisite toys and furnishings of your modern millionaire pro athlete. But he'd grown up poor in the bleak Skyline neighborhood of San Diego, a place beset by violence, drugs, and gangs.

A place not so different, he knows, from the blighted streets of West Baltimore a few miles north of here, the epicenter of the current trouble.

How did it get this bad?

Start with this: relentless poverty. No jobs for young people. Rundown schools with besieged teachers and administrators. Police Athletic League rec centers shuttered for lack of funds. Meaning kids had nothing to do after classes except hurry home over trash-strewn sidewalks and watch the mind-numbing crap on TV, or hang out in the streets, where absolutely nothing good ever happens.

You could add this to the mix, too: block after block of cigarette billboards and liquor stores and bail bond offices, but nowhere to buy fresh fruit and vegetables. Boarded-up row houses. Decrepit playgrounds tagged with gang graffiti and littered with broken glass.

Parks taken over by vacant-eyed junkies slumped on benches, where you needed to step around the discarded needles and condoms to get to the slide or the swing set.

Now take something like what happened with Freddie Gray, re-enforcing a perception of systemic police brutality toward poor people of color, and it was like taking a match to a fuse. That's all it took—*BOOM!*—for a community with no hope to explode.

No, the question was never: How could it happen in Baltimore?

The real question was: How come it didn't happen more often?

Like, oh, every six months or so.

When Jones finally reaches Camden Yards he can hardly believe his eyes. When has he ever seen the ballpark look so quiet and forlorn on a game day?

No crowds milling outside the gates. No food and T-shirt vendors lining the sidewalks. No scalpers working the no-man's-land between the Hilton hotel and Camden Street, watching for the cops out of one eye while hustling the rubes from out of town with cries of, "Who needs tickets? Best seats in the house here!"

No light rail trains squealing to a stop and disgorging thousands of excited fans from the surrounding counties.

Eutaw Street, the stadium's main concourse, is deserted, save for a lone TV cameraman pointing his lens at . . . what? Jones doesn't have a clue. There's not a soul in sight. Not a damn thing going on.

What could the guy be shooting for his station?

Even at this early hour there would normally be smoke billowing from Boog's Barbecue, the popular stand run by former Orioles great Boog Powell that specializes in pit beef, pork, and turkey sandwiches. And employees would already be bustling in and out of the Orioles' team merchandise store and Dempsey's Brew Pub & Restaurant, the joint partly owned by another big-name O's player from back in the day, Rick Dempsey.

Now Jones swings the Raptor around the ballpark, gazing at the jeeps, Humvees, and other military vehicles parked alongside the road, some with exhausted soldiers who've pulled all-night duty sleeping next to them.

There are even tanks here, for God's sake!

Tanks!

And the damned things were all over the news last night, with footage of a couple of them rumbling through the blighted Sandtown-Winchester neighborhood a few miles northwest as though it were an Al-Qaeda stronghold.

As he pulls into the players' parking lot, easing the Raptor past the other shiny trucks, Escalades, Navigators, and Benzes already here, he still has no idea what message he'll deliver to the journalists he'll soon be addressing.

He powers down the windows, kills the engine, and drinks in the silence. He tries to remember the last time he'd played baseball with not a soul in the stands.

Some AAU tournament out in the boonies?

A back-lot spring training game?

A scorching Arizona Fall League contest back in 2003 that not even the geezers with their high-riding Bermuda shorts and noses slathered with zinc oxide bothered to attend?

Naw, there was always *somebody* watching.

Even if it was somebody slumped in a folding chair down the foul line with arms crossed, looking bored out of his mind. Or maybe somebody perched on a corner of the bleachers half-following the game while reading the newspaper, or talking on a cellphone, or whatever.

But there was always *somebody* there.

Now he gets out of the car and feels the warm sunshine on

his face. The sky is so blue it could hurt your eyes. A gentle breeze ripples the flags at the Russell Street entrance. The infamous Baltimore humidity, which can make the town feel like it's wrapped in a damp woolen blanket, is nowhere to be found.

It's a great day for baseball, Adam Jones thinks. *At least if you could blot out the ugliness of all that's happened here.*

But who in their right mind could do that?

He sighs and grabs his bag and walks silently down the ramp into the stadium.

Man, he thinks, *this is gonna be so freakin' weird . . .*

1

THE TRAGIC SAGA OF Freddie Gray begins a little over two weeks earlier on a forlorn corner of West Baltimore notorious for drug activity.

Early on the morning of April 12, unseasonably warm in the city, four police officers on bicycle patrol attempt to stop Gray and another man in the Sandtown-Winchester neighborhood. The cops will say Gray made eye contact and fled "unprovoked."

After a brief chase Gray gives up and is arrested near the Gilmor Homes, a dilapidated public housing project nearby. No drugs are found in his pockets. A knife, though, is. He's placed facedown on the sidewalk and handcuffed.

Cell phone video produced later will show Gray yelling in pain as he's dragged to a waiting transport van, his legs seemingly limp. At some point he asks for an inhaler. He's placed in the back of the van as a crowd gathers and nervous officers hasten to leave the scene.

Gray is already well known to law enforcement officials as a street-level drug dealer and lookout, having been arrested more than fifteen times on various narcotics-related charges. A lead-paint poisoning victim as a child, with parents who themselves were drug abusers, he's a high school dropout caught up in the familiar inner-city cycle of poverty, incarceration, and dead-end prospects for legitimate employment.

What happens next inside the van is not entirely known.

The odds are that it will never be.

Police will deny accusations that he was given a "rough ride," a form of punishment for giving cops a hard time that involves having a handcuffed prisoner tossed about helplessly on the floor of the van while the driver swerves and corners erratically.

The driver of the van will say that Gray was "acting irate."

At one point the van stops and, after police complete paperwork, Gray is placed in leg irons.

When, after making several stops, the van arrives at the Western District police station some forty-five minutes later, Gray is found unconscious. He is treated by paramedics and finally taken to the University of Maryland Shock Trauma Center, where he is diagnosed with a severed spine.

For a week he lies in a coma as the first protests against police brutality begin outside the Western District station. Police defend their handling of the Gray arrest and deny using excessive force. But while the initial protests remain peaceful, the fury of the crowds seems to increase daily.

On the morning of April 19, despite two surgeries in an attempt to save his life, Gray takes his last breath.

He thus joins Eric Garner in Staten Island, New York; Michael Brown in Ferguson, Missouri; Tamir Rice in Cleveland; and Walter Scott in North Charleston, South Carolina, on the ever-growing list of African Americans who have died recently following questionable encounters with police officers.

A prominent Baltimore attorney representing the Gray family delivers a scathing indictment of the police handling of the case.

"What we know is that while in police custody for committing no crime—for which they had no justification for making the arrest except he was a black man running—his spine was virtually severed, 80 percent severed in the neck area," William "Billy" Murphy Jr. says.

Now the protests in Baltimore increase in scope and intensity.

They move to police headquarters and to City Hall downtown. Seething residents are joined by Black Lives Matter organizers, with many in the crowd holding their hands in the air and shouting, "Don't shoot!" at officers keeping a wary watch.

The six officers involved in the Freddie Gray arrest and transport are identified and suspended. The U.S. Department of Justice will also open a criminal and civil rights investigation into Gray's death.

Coming so soon after the chokehold death of Eric Garner and the fatal shootings of Michael Brown, Tamir Rice, and Walter Scott, the Gray case ignites a national furor.

Little wonder that droves of media begin pouring in, eager to cover this fresh tumult in a city already portrayed as bleak, murderous, and drug-riddled on every program from national news shows to podcasts (*Serial*), documentaries ("Baltimore: Anatomy of an American City"), and award-winning HBO dramas (*The Wire, The Corner*).

On Friday, April 24, city officials hold a news conference at which police commissioner Anthony Batts acknowledges that serious mistakes were made by his officers during Gray's arrest.

The prisoner was not buckled properly in a seat belt in the transportation van, Batts says. Nor was he provided timely medical attention on several occasions during the arrest and ride to the police station.

With angry protests entering their sixth day and organizers planning a massive demonstration the following afternoon that will, in the words of one, "shut the city down," there is a growing fear among many that the simmering tensions are about to boil over.

Governor Larry Hogan has already sent state troopers to help the Baltimore police with any potential unrest. And Batts, Mayor Stephanie Rawlings-Blake, and other community leaders are pleading for the protests to remain nonviolent.

But with activists from out of town expected to join the hundreds of seething demonstrators marching from the Gilmor Homes in Freddie Gray's old neighborhood to a rally at City Hall the next day, there is no telling whether those urgent pleas will be heeded.

2

WHAT NO ONE WANTS is another Ferguson.

The memory of the upheaval that roiled the small Missouri town following the fatal shooting of Michael Brown is still fresh—and all too raw. It was only eight months ago that a moving candlelight vigil for the slain Brown gave way to looting and vandalism, and then pitched battles between protesters and tear-gas-lobbing, rubber-bullet-shooting police that played out on the nightly news and riveted the nation for weeks.

For the first hours of the Saturday march for Freddie Gray, the crowd, which authorities estimate at 1,200, is largely peaceful. Even when rowdy teens begin kicking car doors on their way downtown they're admonished by other protesters to chill and remember the larger purpose of the gathering.

At City Hall it's clear the protests have attracted sympathizers from a number of activist African American organizations throughout the country. But Larry Holmes, a New Yorker with the People's Power Assembly, insists the term "outside agitator" is not the pejorative authorities make it out to be.

"They need a little history," he tells the crowd. "Martin Luther King was an outside agitator. Malcolm X was an agitator. Jesus Christ was an agitator."

Not far away, inside Camden Yards, the Orioles are getting ready to play the Boston Red Sox in the second game of a three-game series. A crowd of over thirty-five thousand is expected to be on hand for the 7:05 p.m. start, including the usual boisterous contingent of "Sawks" fans who pour in from all over when their beloved team visits Baltimore.

When the rally at City Hall ends at about four o'clock a group of protesters estimated at between 750 and 1,000 suddenly descends on the ballpark. They protest peacefully for twenty minutes and leave before the gates open for the game at five o'clock.

But when the protesters return at 6:15 they are in a far uglier mood. As Orioles and Red Sox fans make their way to the ballpark in the midst of the chanting, sign-waving masses, they're quickly hustled inside by nervous police and ushers.

Fifteen minutes later, on Washington Boulevard, the small concrete peninsula near the ballpark that houses three popular bars, the scene quickly becomes chaotic.

As demonstrators march by, the sidewalk is packed with Orioles and Red Sox fans enjoying pregame drinks at tables behind metal barricades. Although some fans express solidarity with the marchers (who are chanting, "Black lives matter!"), some in the two groups begin exchanging jeers.

Soon a volley of bottles and cans is being flung at the bar patrons, some of whom are also attacked by demonstrators.

Nearby, protesters jump on police cars and smash their windows with traffic cones. Trash cans are hurled through store windows. A few stores are vandalized and looted. Bike racks set up as security barriers are thrown at police officers.

But the authorities are prepared for trouble. They've been monitoring social media for days and receiving intelligence reports on the movements of the demonstrators for the past twenty-four hours.

Near the ballpark's main entrance police in riot gear form a three-deep barrier behind bicycle racks in a tense standoff with the crowd. White cops are spit on; called "killers" and "murderers"; and warned, "You can't get away with this!" Black officers are jeered and called "Uncle Tom!"

Yet the officers keep their poise and stand tall amid the abuse, earning plaudits from both their supervisors and fans entering the ballpark, many of whom seem both surprised and shaken by the demonstrations.

"Good luck getting home tonight!" one protester yells to a group of wide-eyed Red Sox fans, who appear to be ruing the great hotel rate and discount airfare that lured them down from New England.

Before the game all eyes in the Red Sox's and Orioles' club-houses are turned to the flat-screen TVs and the disturbing images of the melee taking place outside.

Relief pitcher Darren O'Day is particularly concerned for his wife, FOX News reporter Elizabeth Prann, who is a block away covering the protest.

"People do funny things when they see cameras and micro-phones," O'Day tells reporters. "It's kind of a crazy profession. When you see trouble going on, you have to run towards it and (insert) yourself right in the middle of it. There's definitely times when I've been worried about her on a story. You just never know what's going to happen."

The rest of the Orioles also appear to be uneasy.

Manager Buck Showalter, who earlier in the day had attended a memorial service for his father-in-law in Nashville, arrived late to the ballpark because of all the streets closed off by police.

Now he wonders if he might not be bunking at the ballpark tonight for safety reasons, and also because the Orioles have an early game the next day.

Adam Jones, one of only two African Americans on the team, is thrust into his familiar role—one he embraces grudgingly at times—as the media's go-to interview for all issues pertaining to black America.

Now, after watching the violence taking place outside, he looks grim.

"I understand they are fighting for a good cause," he says of the demonstrators. "I understand, fight for your rights. It's what you should do. But try to be safe and smart about it."

The angry marchers eventually leave and head toward Harborplace, the festival warren of shops and eateries that symbolizes the revival of the city's downtown. Some in the crowd smash more car and store windows. As the mass of demonstrators surges into the intersection of Pratt and Light streets, the main intersection at the Inner Harbor, traffic becomes hopelessly snarled.

A total of thirty-one adults and four juveniles are arrested before the mayhem subsides.

The game begins without incident. But within the hour police infiltrators in the crowd are reporting that the demonstrators plan to return to the ballpark.

Around 9:30 Lt. Dennis Reinhard, the stadium commander of the Baltimore Police Department, is informed that, yes, the protesters appear poised to come back. The unified command at police headquarters orders him to lock the stadium gates.

Orioles executives are apoplectic.

In the twenty-three-year history of Camden Yards this has never been done before.

A meeting is hastily called at the ballpark's fifth-floor emergency operations center. The EOC is dominated by an enormous TV screen, which serves as a state-of-the art security-monitoring system, complete with some 250 stadium and CitiWatch cameras.

Gathered around the large burnished-wood conference table in the middle of the room are Reinhard, Maryland Stadium Authority security head Vernon Conaway Jr., various Orioles executives and PR staffers, and a few of Reinhard's officers.

Traveling in upstate New York, John Angelos, the team's executive vice president and son of owner Peter Angelos, participates via cell phone.

When Reinhard relays his intention to lock down Camden Yards Greg Bader, the Orioles' vice president of communications and marketing, says: "You can't do this!"

"Greg," Reinhard says, "not only can I do it, I'm doing it."

The message is clear: the police department is now in charge. Public safety is at risk. Nobody comes in or out until the threat of danger has passed.

"I suggest you write something for the big screen," Reinhard says.

Meaning: post something on the scoreboard to let fans know of the lockdown and why it's happening.

"What do I write?" asks Kristen Hudak.

The blonde-haired, thirty-two-year-old Hudak is the team's brand-new director of public relations. This is her first big-league job after three and a half years at ESPN as a senior publicist. To say she's feeling a bit overwhelmed is an understatement.

This, of course, is understandable. They don't exactly prepare you for a circle-the-wagons confrontation with hundreds of incensed protesters in a troubled city when you're banging out press releases for the Worldwide Leader.

"Up to you what to write," Reinhard replies. "Just write something."

Reinhard, normally equable, isn't trying to be difficult. But he's a tad on the busy side right now.

For one thing his radio is crackling nonstop with updates on the demonstrators' whereabouts. And every five seconds, it seems, he's besieged with another urgent request for info as to what's going on from one of the dozens of officers at the ballpark under his command.

Not only doesn't he have the time to sit and craft a statement for the PR staff, it's not exactly listed in his job description, either.

Thus it is that in the seventh inning an ominous message flashes on the scoreboard screen: "Due to an ongoing public safety issue, the mayor of Baltimore and the Baltimore Police Department have asked all fans to remain in the ballpark until further notice."

The gates are locked and police prepare for more violence. Some fans gathered near the gates who attempted to leave early grumble at the mandate. One man implores an officer to tell Reinhard that the man must leave because his wife has gone into labor.

"No!" Reinhard barks when the message is relayed. "Tell him he shouldn't have come to the game."

That's probably a career-ender, the veteran cop thinks of his brusque reply. But maybe not. Reinhard doesn't believe the man is telling the truth anyway.

Who brings his wife to a ballgame when she's ready to deliver at any moment? It's got to be bullshit.

On the other hand, if an ambulance screams up to the gates soon and paramedics start hovering over the woman and the first cries of a new-born pierce the din . . . well, it's a chance he has to take.

It's simply too dangerous for the police to allow fans, many of them all beered up, many from out of town and unfamiliar with their surroundings, to wander the streets with hundreds of furious demonstrators headed this way.

In a stroke of good fortune for Reinhard and his men, however, a cool rain soon begins to fall.

The game goes into extra innings. But even before outfielder David Lough hits a dramatic walk-off homer in the tenth inning for a 5–4 Orioles win, Reinhard receives word that the rain-soaked demonstrators, previously just blocks away in the Inner Harbor, have dispersed.

The lockdown is lifted. Fans are free to leave. The Red Sox head back to their hotel; the Orioles head home to their families or girlfriends. Buck Showalter is relieved not to have to crash in his cramped office for the night, staring up at the large whiteboard that lists all the Orioles' players until sleep finally comes.

But the eruption outside the ballpark in what had been a week of angry but law-abiding protests has shaken team officials, city leaders, and residents alike.

That night Fredericka Gray, the twin sister of Freddie Gray, delivers a heartfelt plea to the demonstrators while standing next to an exhausted-looking Mayor Stephanie Rawlings-Blake at a hastily called news conference.

"Can y'all please, please stop the violence?" she says, looking down at the words typed on her cellphone before staring wide-eyed into the TV cameras.

Her fallen brother, she insists, would have wanted no part of the destruction, which Rawlings-Blake is blaming on "a small group of agitators." The police, too, are saying it was mainly caused by "isolated pockets of people from out of town."

Another speaker, the Reverend Jamal Bryant, pastor of Empowerment Temple AME Church and a well-known community leader, exhorts all Baltimoreans to "go to your houses of faith" the next day and to "be angry, but sin not."

A short while later another remarkable event takes place: John Angelos eschews the cautious no-comment attitude taken by most top executives when their teams are involved in any kind of crisis or controversy.

After hearing about the unrest while driving with his wife, Margaret, on a darkened stretch of the New York Thruway, and then seeing comments on Twitter about how the violence disrupted fan enjoyment of the game and should not be tolerated, Angelos politely, but pointedly, injects himself in the conversation.

In a ruminative series of twenty-one late-night tweets, the forty-seven-year-old Angelos, who up to this point has maintained a low profile with the club, emerges as a strong populist voice.

Yes, he agrees with many weighing in on Twitter that "the rule of law is of utmost importance in any society."

But he quickly goes on to defend those who protest peacefully, pointing to lost jobs shipped out of the country by "the American political elite" for the "economic devastation" caused to middle-class and working-class families in Baltimore and so many other U.S. cities.

His tweets are instantly embraced by many African Americans and white progressives, both in Baltimore and across the country.

Whether any of this—Fredericka Gray's plaintive cry for peace, John Angelos's social media empathy, or the good reverend's pleas for Baltimoreans to call on God for help—serves as a calming influence is hard to gauge.

But Baltimore is relatively quiet the following day.

At a funeral home in Govans, a northeast Baltimore neighborhood, family, relatives, and total strangers file by the silky-white casket of Freddie Gray to pay their last respects.

"There lay the slim body of Freddie Gray, dressed in a white baseball cap, spotless sneakers, blue plaid tie," Julie Scharper writes for the *Baltimore Sun*. "His boyish face appeared at peace—a sharp contrast to the events that precipitated and have followed his death."

Yet the scene is not exactly peaceful outside.

Demonstrators fill the streets. Some chant, "Hands up! Don't shoot!" Some wave signs expressing solidarity with the Gray family as passing motorists lean on their horns and call for justice for the dead man.

As city council president Bernard C. "Jack" Young leaves the chapel and sees the angry faces outside, he beats back a sense of foreboding and tells reporters, "I'm hoping we can all remain peaceful."

At Camden Yards, five miles to the south, the Orioles hold their annual Little League Day without incident. Young ballplayers in their team uniforms happily parade around the field before the game and trade high-fives with the Orioles and the Oriole Bird mascot.

The crowd is smaller than usual for this highly anticipated event, no doubt in reaction to the ugly images of ballpark mayhem that dominated the TV news the night before. But among the fans who do show up the mood is celebratory.

The Orioles respond in kind with an 18–7 thumping of the Red Sox, instilling hope that they might post another ninety-six-win season and repeat as American League East champions.

At City Hall and at Baltimore police headquarters there is an almost audible sigh of relief when the day passes without major trouble in the streets.

Spring is in the air. The sidewalks downtown are filled with people enjoying the sunny, sixty-four-degree weather, thrilled to be out of the house after the long, cold winter.

For some twenty-four hours, at least, much of Baltimore is living up to its famous nickname, "Charm City."

It's a nickname critics have snickered at for years, given the laundry list of urban ills with which the city struggles.

"Harm City" is more like it, they say.

But as the happy postgame throngs stream from Camden Yards and the Inner Harbor bustles with activity, only the biggest of killjoys would bring that up now.

3

YET BY MONDAY, APRIL 27, the tension in the city is palpable once more as Freddie Gray's funeral gets under way.

Thousands pack New Shiloh Baptist Church in West Baltimore and parade somberly past Gray's open casket, now featuring a white pillow with a screened photo of him smiling serenely.

Large floral arrangements adorn the pulpit. A velvet rope keeps mourners from getting too close. On the two walls on either side of the cavernous room video screens flash alternating messages: "Black Lives Matter" and "All Lives Matter."

In death there is no shortage of dignitaries on hand for the slight young man from the projects who, in life, led such a troubled existence.

The Reverend Jesse Jackson is here. So are Maryland congressmen Elijah E. Cummings and John Sarbanes. Kweisi Mfume, the former Maryland congressman and NAACP president, is here too, along with Mayor Stephanie Rawlings-Blake and representatives from President Barack Obama's White House.

So is eighty-two-year-old Dick Gregory, the legendary comedian and civil rights activist, who has recently been immortalized with a star on the Hollywood Walk of Fame.

Paying their respects too are family members of other young African American men killed after tense encounters with law enforcement officials.

The daughter of Eric Garner, the Staten Island chokehold victim, is in the house, along with the sister of Trayvon Martin, the seventeen-year-old whose death three years earlier at the hands of a Hispanic neighborhood watch volunteer sparked yet another national debate about racial profiling and "stand your ground" laws.

Also here to offer support is the mother of Amadou Diallo, the twenty-three-year-old Guinean immigrant shot forty-one times by police in the Bronx in 1999 after being mistaken for a rape suspect.

Unbeknownst to most in the massive crowd at New Shiloh, just moments before the funeral gets under way the police put out a news release. It says they've received a "credible threat" that three notorious gangs, the Bloods, Crips, and Black Guerilla Family, "have entered into a partnership to 'take out' law enforcement officers."

Within hours police will downgrade the threat as "uncorroborated." But as word of the initial news release filters from downtown to the venerable church at North Monroe Street, tensions are ratcheted up even further.

After a swaying choir delivers a lilting rendition of "Amazing Grace" and other gospel hymns, one speaker after another offers condolences to the Gray family and pleas for peace and unity. They also voice an unwavering certainty that the young man in the starched white shirt, lying in repose at the foot of the pulpit, did not die in vain.

Jesse Jackson will call Freddie Gray a "martyr" and end his remarks with his signature plea: "Keep hope alive!"

But underneath all the lofty rhetoric a not-so-quiet anger simmers.

"With everything that we've been through, ain't no *way* you can sit here and be silent in the face of injustice!" the Reverend Jamal Bryant thunders in his eulogy.

William H. "Billy" Murphy, the Gray family attorney, takes to the podium and expands on the themes of civil rights and the mistreatment of African Americans at the hands of the police.

"Most of us are not here because we knew Freddie Gray," he begins. "We're here because we know too many Freddie Grays. Too many. And you're not here because you grieve for Baltimore, although you do. You're here because you grieve for a nation.

"The eyes of the country are all on us," he continues. "'Cause they want to see whether we got the stuff to make this right. They want to know whether our leadership is up to the task. They want to know whether we're going to act as one people, instead of a community divided by the superficialities of race."

What needs to be gotten right, he adds, is a police culture seemingly devoid of accountability.

"Let's don't kid ourselves," he says. "We wouldn't be here today if it wasn't for video cameras. Instead of one cover-up behind the blue wall after another cover-up behind the blue wall . . . and one lie after another lie, now we see the truth as never before. It's not a pretty picture."

When the service ends the scene outside the church is chaotic.

As pallbearers bring Gray's casket out to the hearse, burly security officials attempt to hold back the shouting crowd pressing in all around them.

It's as if all of West Baltimore is clamoring for a final look at one of their own, the tragic figure whose death has triggered yet more national soul-searching about the long odds faced by young black men reared in poverty.

From New Shiloh the funeral cortege travels to nearby Woodlawn Cemetery and Chapel, led by members of a local motorcycle club.

Some forty-five minutes later, as weeping women, including Gray's mother, Gloria Darden, open white baskets and release doves that flutter into the cloudless sky, cries of "Pepper! Pepper!"—Gray's nickname—fill the air.

A representative from the funeral home says a final prayer. Only then is Gray's casket slowly lowered into the warm, moist earth.

As a few dozen friends and family members file slowly back to their cars and the roar of the departing motorcycles echoes through the tombstones, it's unknowable whether Freddie Gray now rests in peace.

But the city in which he lived—the city that has spawned so many generations of lost Freddie Grays—will have no such luck.

4

THE FIRST SIGN OF trouble comes earlier that same day, when police and city officials begin picking up a strange posting on social media:

All High Schools Monday
@3 We Going to Purge
From Mondawmin, to the Ave,
Back to Downtown #fdl

The reference, authorities discover, is to a 2013 dystopian film, *The Purge*, starring Ethan Hawke. The premise is that all crime, including murder, is deemed legal for one terrifying night each year, during which decent citizens cower behind locked gates as marauding gangs of miscreants rule the streets.

In Baltimore's case the "purge" appears to be organized by high school students. It's scheduled to start at three o'clock in the afternoon at Mondawmin Mall on the city's west side. After that the students plan to march down Pennsylvania Avenue to the Inner Harbor.

Exactly what they plan to do on this march is unclear. But skittish city fathers are unwilling to take any chances. No one can blame them. Accompanying the postings is a photo of two men standing atop a damaged police car surrounded by celebrating Freddie Gray demonstrators, a shot taken two nights earlier during the chaos near Camden Yards.

Local businesses are quickly alerted; many begin shutting down immediately. The University of Maryland –Baltimore cancels classes even though it's finals week. Historic Lexington Market, which dates back to 1782 and is just six blocks from Camden Yards, closes its doors.

Police don riot gear—which many will say later only inflames the situation—and assemble near the mall, where some five thousand students from several area schools normally converge to take buses or the Metro subway home.

Sometime before three o'clock a large group of students walks out of nearby Frederick Douglass High School in protest of Freddie Gray's death, chanting, "Hands up, don't shoot!" The students begin throwing rocks, bottles, and bricks at police, who scramble to protect themselves with their riot shields.

An ill-advised decision by city officials to shut down public transit has even more students trapped near the mall. Unable to get home, they join in the unrest. The ranks of the protesters quickly swell.

As the crowd moves south toward the blighted area of North and Pennsylvania Avenues, the skirmishes devolve into running battles between cops and demonstrators down side streets. Empty police cars are burned. The scene quickly grows more and more anarchic.

Soon police and news helicopters are buzzing overhead. The cops break out Mace and tear-gas and shoot beanbags at the protesters. A few officers, bloodied by flying projectiles, are escorted away for medical treatment.

A police tactical vehicle lumbers into the fray, a steel-armored behemoth called a BearCat with blast-resistant floors, gun ports, and roof hatches. Onlookers will say it looks like something straight out of the war with ISIS.

They're not far off the mark. In fact Bearcat stands for Ballistic Engineered Armored Response Counter Attack Truck. It's become the workhorse for law enforcement and military forces all over the world. And now it's being used to quell an unruly mob of high school students.

Yet it's in the area of North and Penn, a few miles north of the ballpark, that this latest paroxysm of rage enters its most terrifying phase.

Now the violence is unrelenting. More police cars, along with other vehicles, are torched. Stores are looted; a few shopkeepers are threatened and assaulted. Some rioters cover their faces with shirts and bandanas; others see no need to conceal their identity and mug freely—even joyfully—for the television cameras.

As images of the mayhem flash on CNN later that afternoon, an incredulous Wolf Blitzer remarks: "I'm sure viewers around the world are watching and asking: 'Where are the police? Why is this happening? How is this happening in Baltimore?'"

The absence of a strong police response is puzzling to many, who wonder why cops appear to be standing by and allowing the violence to escalate. Equally bewildering is the lack of communication from Mayor Stephanie Rawlings-Blake.

For some reason Rawlings-Blake, who has been on the

job nearly five years, fails to brief city officials and does not hold a press conference on the uprising until some five hours after it starts.

The looting and burning of the Penn North CVS pharmacy, captured in horrifying detail on the cable and network news feeds, will become the defining image of the Freddie Gray unrest.

The first of the looters crashes through the doors in late afternoon. For what seems like an eternity men and women can be seen emerging from the store carrying diapers, soda bottles, paper towels, shampoo, and prescription drugs, among other things.

(Police will soon report their fears that dozens of pharmacies throughout the city have been looted, flooding the illegal drug market with a vast supply of powerful opioids that will cause a dramatic spike in street crime.)

One especially enterprising CVS ransacker is seen casually pushing a shopping cart filled with stolen goods around the corner. Soon the store is torched and thick clouds of dark smoke billow from its rooftop as firefighters arrive to battle the blaze and a phalanx of helmeted police finally marches down Pennsylvania Avenue, attempting to clear it.

Then for many viewers comes the most dispiriting image of all: as a firefighter attempts to connect a hose to a hydrant two masked men are seen running up to the hose and jabbing it with knives, rendering it virtually useless.

When police attempt to move in, clusters of young men throw bricks and bottles. Others roam the streets with pipes and clubs and baseball bats.

Taken together the images paint a stark picture of a big city spiraling out of control, a feckless police department, and an unprepared, indecisive leadership powerless to stop the violence.

African American politicians, church ministers, and groups like the Nation of Islam are already taking to the streets in an effort to calm the situation. Even gang members are calling for peace. A group of older men wearing the signature blue colors of the Crips are seen quietly urging some in the crowd to go home.

Pastor Jamal Bryant, who had eulogized Freddie Gray hours earlier, vows to send men from his church to help defuse the situation. Surveying the damage and the howling bedlam all around him, he sounds both disbelieving and disgusted.

"I'm asking everybody to go home and clear the streets," he says, encircled by a group of jittery-looking reporters. "This is *not* what the [Gray] family asked for, today of all days. The family was very clear that today was a day of sacred closure in the funeral."

But more than a few Baltimoreans are already echoing the thought of city council president Bernard "Jack" Young.

Young, sixty, says the uprising—while confined right now to a smaller swath of the city—reminds him of the 1968 riots that erupted in Baltimore following the assassination of Rev. Martin Luther King.

Those riots in parts of East and West Baltimore lasted eight days. They left six dead, over seven hundred injured, some one thousand small businesses destroyed, and nearly four thousand people arrested. The riots hastened wave after wave of "white flight" to the suburbs. And many parts of the city, where black businesses had thrived, took years to recover—or never recovered at all.

Now Young and his colleagues are praying the same awful scenario doesn't play out again.

And as the violence and burning rage on with seemingly no end, it feels as if all of Baltimore City is praying with them.

5

A FEW MILES SOUTH, as the Orioles and Chicago White Sox gather at Camden Yards for the first of a three-game series, all eyes in both clubhouses turn to the TVs and the mayhem at North and Penn.

Now there are reports that bands of rioters are moving through the center of the city and toward the Inner Harbor, smashing store windows, kicking in security gates, and roughing up frightened passersby. Break-ins and looting are also said to be taking place at Mondawmin Mall.

Most of the moneyed young players on the Orioles' roster have never set foot in the dreary neighborhoods of West Baltimore. Before batting practice they pepper local reporters with questions:

"What are you hearing about the riots?"

"Where's this Mondawmin place, anyway?"

"How close are we to that CVS that's on fire?"

The White Sox are equally transfixed by what they're seeing of the turmoil; the images of thick, black plumes of smoke billowing into the sky, frenzied looting, and street battles with police are something most have never witnessed.

"I think I can speak for all of us. It's a little scary," outfielder Adam Eaton tells reporters. His manager, Robin Ventura, adds: "It's concerning to everyone. Anytime it becomes a violent protest, everyone's on high alert."

Batting practice has a different feel to it as police and news choppers whirr across the sky and the wail of emergency vehicle sirens is heard in the distance. Far fewer fans than normal are making their way through the gates for tonight's game.

Many have been following the wall-to-wall coverage of the unrest, which has now reached Defcon 3 levels, and have been scared away. Others who planned to take light rail are being told that service from north of the city has already been shut down as a precaution.

Rob Manfred, the newly named commissioner of Major League Baseball, is at the ballpark. This is purely a coincidence; Manfred is on a junket to visit all thirty teams to introduce himself, listen to club and player concerns, and talk about issues such as the pace of play.

But now that he's here he's quickly sucked into the growing crisis facing the city and the dilemma facing the Orioles.

Do they try to get this game in and possibly jeopardize the safety of fans and everyone else in the ballpark with an ugly riot going on just a few miles away?

Or do they postpone the game—and maybe the next few as well if the unrest continues—and cause a scheduling nightmare that could disrupt baseball for months?

Team officials have been monitoring the trouble all afternoon. They've been in contact with Manfred, the police, the mayor's office, and the Maryland Stadium Authority, which manages and maintains Camden Yards and M&T Bank Stadium, where the football Ravens play.

Finally, around 5:45, a decision is made: the game will be postponed.

A makeup date will be announced later.

Now, receiving fresh bulletins about rioters headed downtown, the police act to quickly clear the ballpark.

An announcement is made: fans are urged to leave posthaste. So is the media. The White Sox depart immediately for their hotel, the massive, charmless Hilton that rises like an East European housing project just beyond the ballpark's left-field wall.

It's literally just across the street from Camden Yards. But when a group of White Sox announce their intention to walk back, the police offer to provide an escort.

No thanks, say a few of the Sox. They joke that they'll bring their bats for protection.

As the Orioles mill about their clubhouse, changing into their street clothes with one eye on the coverage of the unrest, Buck Showalter comes in from his office.

He looks preoccupied—and this time it has nothing to do with trying to fill out the batting order.

"You guys need to get out of here," the manager says. "Don't hang around. Get with your families."

Most of the Orioles live downtown during the season. What they hear next from club officials is not exactly reassuring.

Go straight home, they're told. Lock your doors. If you want to stay up, fine, that's up to you. But do *not* answer the door.

As the words sink in Chris Davis, the team's slugging first baseman, shoots Adam Jones a look.

The look says: *Wow, this is serious.*

"Dude," Jones tells him, "this is years and years and years of pent-up emotion and frustration coming out for these people in the streets."

Between the turmoil he's seeing on television and the tense expressions on the faces of the stadium cops, Davis suddenly feels vulnerable. And he's far from the only one in the clubhouse who feels this way. He gets the same vibe from his buddy, relief pitcher Tommy Hunter, when they talk.

"As soon as I get home," Hunter says, "I'm getting my stuff out."

There is no confusion in Davis's mind as to what Hunter means by "stuff."

The two men were teammates on the Texas Rangers for three years, and both arrived in Baltimore in 2008 as part of the same trade package for former Orioles starter Koji Uehara.

Now their families live directly across the hall from each other in a luxury apartment complex in Canton, a waterfront neighborhood on the city's southeast side.

Davis is from Texas. Hunter is from Indiana. But both embrace the shooting culture so dominant in their home states. The reference to "stuff" is clear: Hunter plans to pull out his guns the minute he walks in the door.

Interpret the Second Amendment any way you want, Hunter seems to be saying. But a man needs to protect his family at a time like this.

Listening to his buddy, Davis thinks: *Maybe I should do the same thing.*

No, the unrest has not yet spread to Canton. Despite the increasingly disturbing images from Penn North flickering on the big-screen TVs in the funky bars like Looney's Pub and Nacho Mama's that line the Square, plenty of customers are still knocking back beers and Orange Crushes.

But it's still early. Who knows what the long night ahead might bring?

One Oriole who does not seem terribly concerned at all when leaving the stadium is Adam Jones. On the way to his car, after the third or fourth white policeman tells him, "Stay safe out there!" Jones suppresses a laugh.

Hey, he thinks, *I'm a black man! They're not going to do anything to me! I might even roll the windows down on the way home. Now maybe YOU should be the one who stays safe out there!*

On the other hand Caleb Joseph, the Orioles' twenty-eight-year-old catcher, finds himself getting more and more jittery about reports that the rioters are headed downtown. Joseph lives in the Locust Point neighborhood of South Baltimore with his wife, Brooke, and their infant son, Walker.

With All-Star Matt Wieters on the disabled list following elbow surgery, Joseph has been thrown into the breach as his replacement, which is nerve-wracking enough. In his first full season with the big-league team after six years in the Minors, the native of Franklin, Tennessee (pop. 74,794), is also still getting used to life in the big city of Baltimore.

Now he wonders if he might also have to deal with a rampaging mob that might be headed his way.

Within minutes of arriving home from the ballpark, he gets a call from a relative who works in local law enforcement.

"This is serious stuff," the relative says of the protesters. "Right now, it looks like they're moving away from you. But we have no idea where they could go. So stay alert. Stay aware of the situation."

If the rage he's seeing acted out on the streets isn't unsettling enough, the phone call has left him even more jangled. Now he wonders if the upscale commercial stores and restaurants below his apartment might be an inviting target for looters and arsonists.

Nevertheless, even as he and Brooke sit glued to the screen watching the turmoil in the streets, the idea of a riot cancelling a game remains inconceivable to him.

We play in snow. We play in rain. We play in lightning sometimes, he thinks. *Things must really be bad for this game to be called off . . .*

In fact, in many ways things are rapidly getting worse.

Locust Point and Canton and other mostly white neighborhoods will be largely spared from the violence. But in less than two hours the mayor and Gov. Larry Hogan will declare a state of emergency. Both have already spoken with President Barack Obama, who has offered his support.

Hogan will activate the National Guard and troops will begin rolling into the city before midnight to keep the peace. Some five hundred state troopers have been sent to the city and another five thousand police officers from other states will be summoned to keep order as well.

Tuesday classes will be cancelled at all Baltimore schools. Rawlings-Blake, looking hollow-eyed and dispirited, announces that a citywide curfew from 10:00 p.m. to 5:00 a.m. will begin the next day.

All of it will help. But the city has already paid a heavy price for what many feel is decades of neglect of its most desperate citizens.

The mayor's office will report that nineteen buildings and 144 vehicles have been set on fire. More than 380 businesses are damaged or destroyed. Property damage will be estimated at some $13 million.

Over 235 people are arrested. At least twenty police officers are hurt.

And who knows if the worst of it is over?

That's what most consumes Chris Davis in his Brewer's Hill apartment as the night wears on.

Earlier Tommy Hunter had invited him over for a beer. But both men had ultimately decided it was wiser to remain with their own families in case of any trouble.

So now here is Davis, sitting alone in his darkened living room, unable to tear his eyes from the glowing blue-white screen in front of him and the tragedy playing out in the streets of Baltimore.

He and his wife, Jill, had put their infant daughter Ella to bed hours earlier. Then Jill had gone to bed as well. Jill is a nurse—used to seeing a lot of crazy things, Chris knows. But he could see how upset she was by everything she had watched on TV.

The two of them love the city. And to see it torn apart like this hurts them deeply.

"I don't even know what to think about all this," Jill had said, shaking her head over and over. "This is awful."

Chris feels the same way. As the night wears on he becomes more and more melancholy.

Baseball is as far from his thoughts as it can be right now. He's a Christian, outspoken about his faith, a new father at age twenty-nine with a young wife and daughter. Maybe that's why the kind of pain and fury he sees on the faces of the young protesters eats at him so much.

All he knows is this: he feels horrible for Freddie Gray and his family, horrible for the brave police officers who are putting their lives on the line to protect lives and resources, horrible for their families, horrible for everyone involved in this ugliness.

It's late when he picks up his phone and texts his buddy Hunter: "What are you doing?"

A soft ping and there's the reply: "Probably the same thing you're doing. Sitting on the couch. Watching the news. Thinking about what I'm gonna do if something happens here."

Yes, that's what Chris Davis is doing, too.

For a long while he sits there in the dark, two handguns cradled in his lap, watching with alarm as the city boils over, wondering what the rest of the night—and the next day— will bring.

6

AS TUESDAY DAWNS UNSEASONABLY warm and humid, a strange pallor seems to settle over Baltimore.

The unrest has stopped, at least for now. But scorched buildings still smolder at the epicenter of the rioting and blackened, gutted cars litter many streets. Shattered glass from storefront windows is everywhere, as are the rocks, bricks, and bottles that were aimed in fusillades at police last night.

Before noon a decision is made to cancel the Orioles–White Sox game for a second straight night. The city is still too tense. Public safety for a big event downtown cannot be guaranteed. Orioles management and American League officials in New York hold urgent discussions about what to do with tomorrow's game, as well as the coming weekend's three-game home series against the Tampa Bay Rays.

Meanwhile the Orioles take a gamble and schedule a workout at Camden Yards for early that afternoon. The White Sox do the same. Both workouts are closed to the media. In this volatile atmosphere there's no need to attract attention for something as mundane as ballplayers getting in their swings and loosening their arms.

For the Sox the workout is as much a question of preserving their sanity as anything else. They have a serious case of cabin fever, having been stuck in their hotel for the past eighteen hours watching movies and playing video games when not getting updates on the rioting.

When a few players left to get something to eat across the street Monday night they saw helmeted cops with assault weapons wrestling angry protesters to the ground. That was enough to make room service look more and more enticing, and they quickly returned to their hotel.

Around one o'clock, just before leaving his apartment for the Orioles' workout, Davis gets a text from Tommy Hunter, who left fifteen minutes earlier.

"Hey, you need to go through the city today," it says.

Davis texts back: "Everything OK?"

"Yeah," Hunter replies. "Just do it."

So Davis winds his way in from Canton, and when he hits Lombard Street, the Inner Harbor visible on his left through gaps in the office buildings and parking garages, he sees what Hunter is referring to.

He sees dozens of grim-faced National Guard troops wearing camouflage and carrying assault rifles lining the sidewalks—some 1,700 are here already. Their dun-colored assault vehicles can be seen lurching down hushed, deserted streets.

There's a sickly odor in the air, too. It smells like a thick toxic stew of burnt rubber and melted plastic.

But it's when he turns down Conway Street toward the huge red-brick warehouse that forms the signature façade of Camden Yards that the full scope of this civic emergency reveals itself.

Metal barricades are in place, and the vast sea of parking

lots between the ballpark and M&T Bank Stadium, home of the Ravens, has been turned into a staging area.

Military vehicles and troop transport buses are everywhere. So are scores of police cars from the District of Columbia, Pennsylvania, Delaware, Virginia, and New Jersey. Ambulances and paramedics stand at the ready. Huge operational tents and food tables for cops, soldiers, and first-responders dot the sea of asphalt normally taken up by happy tailgating, beer-guzzling sports fans.

The sight is jolting to Davis.

It's like something out of the movies, one of those apocalyptic flicks where a panicked populace braces for the invasion of evil Soviet marauders or godless North Korean troops or vicious aliens from outer space—or maybe all three.

Should I even be here? he wonders, feeling more than slightly disoriented.

But he's here already, so there's no going back. And his entrance, it must be said, does not go unnoticed.

Mainly that's because he's driving a snow-white Ford F-250 with an eight-inch lift on thirty-eight-inch tires, a snorting, belching colossus that looks like something from *Mad Max* meets *Smokey and the Bandit.*

He rolls into the players' parking lot with the windows up and the sound system turned down low, but the gaping from the soldiers and police officers he passes is almost comical.

"You know what they were probably saying?" Hunter jokes later. "'Who's this freakin' redneck pulling up? Is he lost?'"

Despite the lingering sense of unease in the city and the massive show of force in the streets, Baltimoreans begin picking up small signs of hope.

Most businesses downtown are still closed, including the top two tourist attractions, the National Aquarium and Science Center. Federal buildings and city agencies have also shut their doors.

Over in Highlandtown, a traditional blue-collar neighborhood on the east side, reports are coming in that many businesses there were also vandalized and looted, indicating that the unrest had spread quickly to other parts of the city the night before.

But up at Pennsylvania and North avenues, a massive and impromptu cleanup of the riot damage has begun.

Residents, black and white, turn out to shovel debris from the streets, sweep the sidewalks, and haul away plastic bags filled with trash. City public works crews are also on the scene as volunteers wearing work gloves lug charred metal shelves and broken slabs of countertop from the scorched shell of the cvs.

With Mayor Stephanie Rawlings-Blake and Gov. Larry Hogan on a walking tour to assess the destruction, the intersection takes on a festive air as a six-man band plays jazz tunes, people dance in the streets, and others sing and pray for an end to the violence.

The music can't be soothing enough for Rawlings-Blake, who's had a difficult seventy-two hours.

After the vandalism and smashing of police cars near Camden Yards Saturday night, she was heavily criticized for telling the media that city officials had given "space to those who wished to destroy."

By Monday evening she was being ripped for waiting too long to request National Guard assistance from the governor, despite her insistence that calling in the Guard earlier could have escalated the unrest.

Attempting to walk back her "space to destroy" remarks at an earlier news conference, she again seemed to stumble before lashing out at a familiar foe: the media.

"Taken in context," she said defensively, "I explained that, in giving peaceful demonstrators room to share their message, unfortunately, those who were seeking to incite violence also had space to operate."

Yet this clarification quickly gave way to another controversy when she labeled the protesters who had destroyed property "thugs," opening the forty-five-year-old African American mayor—who had recently won an award from the National Congress of Black Women—to curious charges of racism.

"I can tell you: that did not go over well on the streets of Baltimore," Kweisi Mfume says of Rawlings-Blake's language. "She lost a lot of credibility. People didn't like the use of that word."

The mayor was forced to walk back that term, too. But she did it in style, with a bit of self-deprecating humor.

After declaring at a news conference, "We don't have thugs in Baltimore," she added: "Sometimes my own little anger translator gets the best of me."

The reference was to a Key & Peele Comedy Central skit that purported to allow preternaturally composed President Barack Obama to voice his innermost rage and frustration through a doppelganger, played by Keegan-Michael Key. And the line served to humanize Baltimore's embattled mayor to many of her skeptical constituents.

(Ironically Obama had also labeled the rioters "criminals and thugs" when first weighing in on the unrest, a fact that did not go unnoticed—at least privately—by the contrite mayor and her team.)

But walking the streets now, talking quietly with still-nervous residents as the syncopations and polyrhythms of jazz fill the air, Rawlings-Blake seems the very picture of a composed, resolute leader determined to shepherd this city out of its mess.

Her message, simple and direct, is identical to the one she has posted on her Facebook page: "We will clean, we will rebuild, and we will heal."

Yet in this long-troubled neighborhood, which so often seems forgotten by the movers and shakers of this city in their haste to erect ever more shiny monuments to commerce along the waterfront, many wonder if any of that will ever come true.

7

IF AN IMPROMPTU CELEBRATION at Penn North within hours of a fiery civic upheaval seems incongruous, so does the unlikely cult of celebrity growing around a Baltimore woman named Toya Graham.

Graham, a single mother of six, is being called a "Hero Mom" for her actions in the rock-throwing melee near Mondawmin Mall twenty-four hours earlier.

Stunned by the violence she was watching on TV and concerned that her son, sixteen-year-old Michael, might be involved, she raced to the scene of the trouble. Finding him in the middle of the pandemonium wearing a black hoodie with a mask over his face, she admittedly "just lost it."

In a riveting video clip first aired by local station WMAR-TV Graham was seen in a bright yellow shirt and jeans running up to Michael and screaming and pummeling him with her hands and fists.

As the boy tried to walk away Graham's fury seemed only to increase.

"GET THE FUCK OVER HERE!" she yelled, running after him and smacking him again.

"TAKE YOUR MOTHERFUCKING MASK OFF!" she continued, raining more slaps. "YOU GONNA BE OUT HERE DOING THIS DUMB SHIT?"

Finally the tall, lanky boy tore off his mask and stopped.

When he turned to face her he appeared ashamed and embarrassed. And seconds after this confrontation with his mother he loped away from the crowd and headed home. And with that there was one less angry young African American battling the police and putting his life—and the life of the officers being attacked with salvos of stones, bricks, and chunks of cinder blocks—in danger.

"I'm a no-tolerant mother," Graham tells the station. "Everybody who knows me knows I don't play that. He knew. He knew he was in trouble."

Within hours the video of Graham confronting her son goes viral, and the "Hero Mom" finds herself the improbable center of attention. Reaction begins pouring in from all over the country—and the world.

At a press conference that night Baltimore police commissioner Anthony Batts sings her praises: "I wish I had more parents who took charge of their kids tonight."

By Tuesday seemingly every network and cable news show is clamoring for an interview. Anderson Cooper, who calls Graham's actions "tough love," wants her on his show. *Good Morning, America* calls. Whoopi Goldberg invites her to appear on *The View*.

Word even goes out that the High Priestess of All Media, Oprah Winfrey, is attempting to score a sit-down. Political commentator Ben Stein will be so swept up in the hyperbole swirling around Toya Graham that he will go so far as to label her "the Rosa Parks for 2015."

To be sure there are dissenting voices—many of them from whites—who find Graham's language and thumping of her son to be appalling.

Erin Burnett of CNN gingerly tries to raise the subject in an interview with city councilor Carl Stokes, an African American, and Kweisi Mfume, the former Maryland congressman and NAACP head.

"You see her trying to do the right thing," Burnett says after showing a clip of Graham confronting Michael. "Of course she's doing it by being very violent against her son. What's your reaction to what she did?"

"Well, you say violent . . . ," Stokes begins before Mfume quickly interrupts him.

"*Violent*?" Mfume repeats incredulously. "She's trying to tell him"—here he repeatedly slaps one hand against the other for emphasis—"'If . . . you . . . don't . . . get . . . off . . . this . . . street . . . I . . . will . . . drag . . . you . . . home!' Now if that's violence, maybe it's *necessary* violence. And a lot of mothers are reacting that way. And a lot of us grew up with that, so you didn't make the same mistake twice."

Yet for the most part the main narrative being spun is this: Toya Graham is the poor but fiercely proud Baltimore mom determined to protect her family from the poverty, social ills, and despair all around her.

And for that the African American community is roundly applauding her.

As it happens Toya Graham's own personal backstory turns out to be just as inspiring.

She was one of four children who grew up in a tough neighborhood in northwest Baltimore. Her mother died when she was nineteen, and not long after that Toya became hooked on drugs.

She dropped out of high school and later earned her GED. But ensnared in a succession of low-paying jobs and riddled with constant worries about paying the bills, she has led a life of nonstop pain and worry.

Yet all of it, her supporters say, steeled something in her.

So it was, they say, that in a moment of sheer pandemonium, with a city about to detonate and her son and other young black men engaged in a potentially deadly standoff with the police, Toya Graham had the courage and moral clarity to do the right thing.

In one of her first interviews Graham herself provides the fitting coda for her ferocious reaction to finding Michael in the midst of the melee near Mondawmin.

"That's my only son," she tells WMAR, "and at the end of the day, I don't want him to be a Freddie Gray."

On this, one of the saddest days in the city's history, there are hundreds of African American mothers all over Baltimore mouthing the same desperate wish.

8

AROUND ONE O'CLOCK THAT afternoon, even as Toya Graham adjusts uneasily to her newfound fame, the Orioles make an astonishing announcement: with the city still a tinderbox and police needed in the neighborhoods where the unrest has been at its worst, tomorrow's game against the White Sox will be held behind locked gates.

With no fans in attendance.

Furthermore the three upcoming weekend games against Tampa Bay, originally scheduled for Camden Yards, will be moved to Tampa, with the Orioles designated as the home team for the series.

The reaction is instantaneous. City leaders, baseball fans, and the rest of the Major League clubs are nonplussed.

The Orioles are doing what?

Within minutes the club is besieged with requests from news organizations all over the country for credentials to cover this singular contest. The story angle is irresistible: a baseball game in a scarred, riot-torn town that could erupt again at any moment? Okay, that's crazy enough. But the first one ever played without spectators in the 146-year history of the Major Leagues?

What in God's name will that be like?

By late afternoon Greg Bader, the Orioles' veep of communications and marketing, realizes that Wednesday's game will be the biggest event, in terms of media attention, that Camden Yards has ever seen.

Yes, the Orioles have hosted big events before: playoff games and the American League Championship Series, not to mention milestone celebrations like the raucous night in 1995 when the great Cal Ripken Jr. broke Lou Gehrig's record for consecutive games played.

But this will be more like hosting a World Series—except with only twenty-four hours' notice. And without the massive PR staffing normally provided by Major League Baseball to help the home team cope with all the media requests.

Not to mention the fact that, with the city still a powder keg, there would also be none of the fun and pageantry of a Series game. No, there will be no excited throngs passing through the turnstiles at Camden Yards for this one, no beaming celebrities throwing out the first pitch, no fireworks, no red, white, and blue bunting draped over the railings.

Yet as darkness falls on Tuesday and angry demonstrators again begin gathering at North and Penn the Orioles' decision to play behind locked gates the next afternoon looks prescient.

Until this moment the day has been marked by largely peaceful protests, the Great Cleanup, and a general sense of shock and sadness over the level of violence that erupted. An earlier program at the Empowerment Temple AME Church in West Baltimore, with religious leaders of various faiths calling for the city to come together, attracted over a thousand people.

But now hundreds of demonstrators are in the streets as the ten o'clock curfew approaches, and the mood is tense.

From a police helicopter overhead a loudspeaker blares repeated requests for the crowd to go home. But this is largely met with curses and raised fists and bottles thrown at police, even as officers in riot gear shoot tear gas, lob pepper balls, and prepare to clear the streets.

As the protesters become more and more agitated, it's hard to see who bears the brunt of their anger most: law enforcement officials or the hordes of media now being blamed by many for inflammatory coverage of the unrest.

"Why aren't y'all talking about the root causes of all this?" someone shouts at reporters. "Why aren't y'all reporting on the poverty, the lack of jobs, the hopelessness of these young kids?"

At one point a police officer points to a clutch of TV cameras and a familiar figure with a shock of gray hair and a curled mustache clutching a FOX News microphone.

"God help us," the cop mutters. "Geraldo is here."

And yes, there he is, the legendary Geraldo Rivera, who, to no one's surprise, has turned out in all his outsized Geraldo-ness.

Dressed in a hip black mock turtleneck and fashionable eyeglasses, Rivera moves jauntily through the crowd, flashing an incandescent smile as if he were covering a Broadway opening or an inaugural ball.

But when he attempts to interview state senate majority leader Catherine Pugh for a live shot on Sean Hannity's show, he's quickly surrounded by a ring of protesters. And when a young man named Kwame Rose gets in his face, Rivera's breezy grin reverts to an annoyed rictus.

"THIS IS MY CITY!" Rose cries. "THIS IS OUR CITY! WE WANT YOU GONE!"

As the crowd heckles Rivera—"You're making money off of black pain!" a woman yells—Rose moves in front of the camera. For a moment this blocks viewers from what FOX producers surely want them to see most: the fabled newsman bravely dealing with a hostile crowd.

"You're making a fool of yourself!" Rivera snarls.

But Rose will not be put off.

Even as one of the huge FOX News bodyguards shoots baleful looks at him and attempts to block him from Rivera, the twenty-year-old activist with a stylish NBA baller's goatee and cap worn backwards continues berating the veteran journalist.

"I WANT THE WHITE MEDIA OUT OF BALTIMORE CITY!" he shouts. "YOU'RE NOT HERE TO REPORT THE REAL STORY!"

The tense standoff continues for another few seconds. The crowd is becoming more and more agitated.

In the end, though, it is Rivera who finally blinks.

As he and Pugh attempt to move away, Rivera loudly—and, it could be said, unhelpfully—promises Hannity the interview will continue "if we can get her away from these . . . these *vandals* here!"

"They seem like they want trouble," Rivera says to the politician.

With an emphatic shake of her head Pugh replies: "No, they don't want trouble."

But Rivera, as is his wont, ignores this. Instead he opens a new line of interrogation in an attempt to salvage this train wreck of a one-on-one.

"Where do we go from here tonight?" he asks above the din.

"We want our people to go home," Pugh answers calmly. "But we also want the media to move back. This is just inciting people."

In the FOX viewing audience this observation surely elicits a few chuckles.

Geraldo? Inciting people?

Where could anyone get that idea?

After the awkward exchange wraps up, Geraldo and his crew finally leave. And within the hour, as the line of police moves forward rattling riot shields ominously, and black leaders, including Pugh, implore people to "take your babies home," the protesters begin to disperse.

On this night there will mercifully be no repeat of the terrible violence that gripped the city twenty-four hours earlier.

But how long the tenuous calm will last is still anyone's guess.

9

BY EARLY WEDNESDAY, A gorgeous spring day with temperatures headed to the seventies, downtown Baltimore is a tale of two cities.

Look south past the Inner Harbor, across the sparkling blue water to the American flag flying high atop Federal Hill and the upscale townhouses and tidy cobblestone streets, and it's like something from a Chamber of Commerce brochure.

But turn your eyes east toward Pratt Street and the huge police and military presence as far as the eye can see, and the scene is more Operation Desert Storm than "Good Morning Baltimore."

In the middle of it all the charming ballpark that started the "retro" craze in stadium architecture twenty years ago has never looked more forsaken. The main entrance to Camden Yards on Eutaw Street, with its signature statue of Baltimore-born Babe Ruth, is devoid of the usual gameday activity.

The concourses are dark and silent. On the sixty-foot-wide promenade that runs adjacent to the warehouse, normally bustling with pregame activity, store windows are shuttered. Merchandise kiosks are draped in plastic. Bits of old ticket stubs from an overturned trash can swirl lightly in the breeze like tumbleweed.

The question on the minds of all who will be allowed into the ballpark today is this: what will the experience be like?

What will it *feel* like to play in a big-league game in front of zero fans? To *watch* it and report on it from high above in the press box? To *broadcast* it on TV and radio in a setting more reminiscent of a hushed cathedral than a vibrant ballpark with a lively and partisan crowd on hand?

As it turns out even baseball Hall of Famers are seeking the answers to these existential questions.

Orioles executive vice president Dan Duquette discovers this around nine in the morning after doing a live interview with Mike Barnicle of the MSNBC talk show *Morning Joe*. The two have known each other since the mid-1990s, when Duquette was the general manager of the Boston Red Sox and Barnicle was the star columnist with the *Boston Globe*.

The Orioles are attempting to low-key this game in all respects, not wishing for it to detract in any way from the serious business of a city reeling from major civic unrest. But when Barnicle asked Duquette to go on the air to talk about the historical uniqueness of the event, he reluctantly agreed.

When the brief interview wraps up, Duquette turns and sees a familiar figure riding by on a bicycle. It's Orioles legend Cal Ripken Jr., out getting exercise before meeting a friend at a nearby hotel for breakfast.

Baseball's "Iron Man" stops and the two exchange greetings.

Ripken's vaunted career spanned twenty-one seasons in the Major Leagues. He played in every conceivable setting, no matter how challenging. He played in rain, snow, thunder, and lightning. He played in All-Star Games, playoff games, World Series, strike-shortened seasons, on goodwill trips to Japan.

He played sick. He played hurt. He played after being hit by pitches and after vicious home plate collisions. He played after twisting his knee during a nasty brawl with the Seattle Mariners that featured NFL-style tackles near the mound and wild haymakers whistling through the air, instead of the usual harmless pushing and shoving that characterize most baseball fights.

But he's never, ever, played a big game without anyone in the stands.

"I'd like to see what that's like," he tells Duquette.

"Okay, come on by when you're through and we'll watch the game together," Duquette replies.

The Orioles' exec has planned to take in the game in his box with his wife, Amy, and a couple of their kids. But having as his guest the storied ballplayer who shattered Lou Gehrig's record for consecutive games played—a record once deemed unbreakable by just about everyone except the seriously delusional—will not exactly be a downer for the Duquette family.

As the Orioles and White Sox begin drifting into the ballpark Buck Showalter sits in his office and wonders how his team will perform in what will surely be the strangest game he's ever managed.

As it happens, though, the Orioles' manager is not altogether unfamiliar with the concept of a fanless contest.

As a star point guard for his high school basketball team— William Nathaniel Showalter III was known as Nat back then—he once played in a contest against a rival school in a closed gym with only players, coaches, and referees allowed in.

This was in the small Florida Panhandle town of Century. Vicious brawls had broken out in the stands and on the court in previous games between Century High and Flomaton High, just across the nearby Alabama border. Hence the decision to ban students, parents, and cheerleaders the next time the two rivals met.

The Century Blackcats beat the Flomaton Hurricanes that day. Showalter doesn't remember the final score or how many points he had. But what he *does* remember are the sounds of that game: the labored breathing and grunts as players fought through picks or went up for rebounds, the squeaking of sneakers on the polished floor, the PFFFT! of the ball ripping through the net after a long jump shot—all of it sounding so magnified in the small, empty gym.

There was a purity to the whole affair that Nat Showalter appreciated: no crazed moms and dads yelling at their sons to shoot or hustle or play defense. No players flexing and showing off for their girlfriends.

No one in the bleachers jeering at the other team, hoping

to start trouble and maybe even a donnybrook for the ages in the parking lot afterward.

It was just basketball. The game returned to its very essence. Our five on the court versus your five. Lock the doors and let's see who's better.

Will this game with the White Sox be anything at all like that? he wonders as he goes through his usual meticulous pregame preparations.

Yet of more pressing concern to the manager now is this terrible upheaval in the city and the seemingly intractable issues of race, poverty, and social justice it's stirred up.

As a fifty-eight-year-old white man who grew up in the segregated South of the 1960s he's acutely aware of how this kind of disquiet can tear apart a community.

His father, Bill Showalter, was a World War II hero and high school principal who was also an ardent proponent of integration. While Buck often speaks of a carefree upbringing in Century, which he's likened to Mayberry, the sleepy fictional hamlet depicted on TV's *Andy Griffith Show*, racial attitudes in a sleepy sawmill town were hardly enlightened.

Bill and Lina Showalter, Buck's mom, had no patience for bigotry though. If you sat at Lina's dinner table and uttered a single untoward word about blacks she'd silence you with a glare that could freeze blood in the veins.

From all accounts Bill Showalter was an independent-minded man whose ethical stands rankled many in the community.

Once, when his teachers walked off the job to protest working conditions, he walked off with them, despite warnings that he'd never work in the school system again. Yet when the schools were finally integrated it was Bill Showalter who was tapped to be the principal of the formerly all-black middle school.

The following Sunday, Buck recounts with pride, his dad loaded up the car with Lina, Buck, and his three sisters and drove over to Pilgrim Lodge Baptist Church, where blacks in the town worshipped.

As the family walked through the doors the entire congregation turned and stared in wonder. At some point during the service Bill Showalter got up and gave a stirring talk about unity and about how the integration of the schools was the best thing that could have happened to Century.

Buck sat in one of the cramped pews, listening in amazement.

"I had never seen my dad talking like that!" he would say years later, voice filled with pride.

Bill Showalter would go on to hire the preacher, a man named Willie Carter, to be the guidance counselor at his new school. The church secretary, Edith Paige, was offered a job there too.

But while Bill Showalter's stature in the black community grew enormously, none of this set well with some of the more intolerant citizens of Century.

Buck still remembers the late-night phone calls that would come to the house, sharp voices asking his dad just what in the hell he was doing, others hissing at him in the darkness to watch his ass because something might happen to his family.

Ever since those days Buck Showalter has studied the intersection of race and society the way he's studied the game of baseball: thoroughly, passionately, with Talmudic rigor.

Even though a fitful calm has settled over Baltimore this morning, he's worried that the violence isn't over, that one more incident could trigger another wave of unrest that would divide the city even further.

Plus, he knows, the police report on how Freddie Gray died is due to come out in just two days.

How will the city react to that?

Will the ransacking and burning happen all over again?

It saddens him just thinking about the prospect of more chaos.

What's troubling Showalter, too, is the look of anguish he's seeing on the face of the Orioles' owner, Peter Angelos, a man he's grown to respect enormously.

Showalter managed three different teams—the New York Yankees, Arizona Diamondbacks, and Texas Rangers—before arriving in Baltimore. At each stop he earned a reputation as a wizard who could quickly turn losing teams into winners, but one who could also wear out his welcome with an overbearing, control-freak nature.

A 2014 profile of Showalter by author Pat Jordan for sportsonearth.com painted him as a baseball version of Captain Queeg and Tony Soprano rolled into one, a characterization that irritates him to no end.

"He hates it because he doesn't consider himself a control freak," Jordan wrote, "but mostly, he hates it because he can't control people calling him a control freak."

But whether he is or isn't obsessive about putting his stamp on a ballclub, the Orioles, Showalter insists, will be his last managing gig.

Most observers feel the two-time Manager of the Year has mellowed considerably and is easier to be around. And he probably gets along better with the front-office types here than anywhere else he's been.

But there's more: he loves the blue-collar vibe of the city and the passion of Orioles fans. He's got a great relationship with the owner too. So to see Angelos, a life-long Baltimorean, torn up by this ruinous strife that has ripped apart his hometown . . . well, it just eats at Showalter. More than almost anything he's experienced.

Showalter was especially impressed with the way Angelos signed off immediately on the idea of playing today's game in a locked stadium, freeing the police to be deployed to the hotspots of this troubled town.

"Mr. Angelos was way ahead on that," Showalter has been telling everyone. "This was something he wanted to do right, regardless of what it would cost him financially. Not once did I hear about the gate and how much it was going to cost the team."

Yet despite how conflicted he's feeling, Showalter knows he must turn his attention to the game that will be played here in a little over three hours.

This is no relaxed spring training exhibition in front of a bunch of beered-up tourists and drowsy retirees in Sarasota. This one counts in the standings.

How do we beat the White Sox? he wonders. *How do we get to Samardzija and that laser of a fastball? Do we have any advantages—any at all—in a stadium that will feel like a library for nine innings?*

Maybe he'll look at the stats again, the ones he got from the advance meeting the Orioles already held on the White Sox.

One thing's for sure: he's won't be giving any rah-rah speeches to his players before they take the field.

I'm not gonna bullshit them, he thinks. *I can't stand up in front of them and give them the deep John Wayne voice and say: "Okay, listen, I've been through this before and here's what's gonna happen . . ."*

Instead, if any of them ask what to expect in this game, he'll probably shrug.

Then he'll tell them the same thing he plans to tell the media when they ask him the same question in an hour or so: "We're in uncharted territory here. Let's go out there and see what happens."

10

IN THE BALTIMORE AND Chicago clubhouses, both uncertainty and nervous anticipation are present in the hours before the first pitch.

Zach Britton, the Orioles' closer coming off a solid thirty-seven-save season, wonders if playing this game is a good idea at all.

Maybe we needed to give the city a little bit more time to deal with everything, he thinks as the Orioles get ready for batting practice.

The rest of the Orioles seem equally ambivalent. Conversations between players are quick and conducted in hushed tones. There's very little joking and even less needling and trash-talking. Not knowing what awaits them in the tomblike quiet of the ballpark has left them devoid of their usual swagger.

Chris Davis senses something else too, an unspoken pressure the Orioles appear to be putting on themselves. It's definitely something he's feeling as well.

We HAVE to win this game, he thinks as he sits in front of his locker and gazes around at his teammates. *We can NOT lose this game. This city needs a win right now. In ANY way possible.*

In the visiting team clubhouse Adam Eaton, the fleet White Sox center fielder, appears equally conflicted. He has just signed a new five-year, $23.5 million deal with the club that has left him energized and even more motivated for the new season.

But being cooped up in his hotel room for days watching the nonstop coverage of the unrest has made him appreciate how volatile the city remains.

"We all just need to get out back out there," he tells reporters who ask about the Sox mindset right now. "But one part of me says this is bigger than baseball. Another part of me says we shouldn't adjust to what people do outside the stadium.

"I'm trying to be as delicate as possible with that," he adds. "But I think normalcy would be good for the people (in) the city."

As Buck Showalter did, Eaton talks about how this fanless game might be baseball stripped down to its essence, no distractions, nine innings enveloped in a throwback vibe. As if it might feel like something out of *Field of Dreams*, minus the traipsing through five-foot stalks of ripening corn to get to the diamond.

Yet as thoughtful and restrained as his remarks are, Eaton will go on to lose his mind just moments later.

That's when he picks up his phone, takes to Twitter and unaccountably writes to his thousands of followers: "We are gonna do our best to take the crowd out of it early. Wish us luck."

It's a joke, of course. And a lame one at that. And maybe it plays well back in Chicago. Maybe a majority of the White Sox faithful even regard it as the very cutting edge of wit and wonder if Eaton has a future in stand-up when he hangs it up for good.

But in Charm City it's way, *way* too soon for jokes.

Things are still too volatile. Too many people are still hurting. Too many others are certain that the lull in the unrest is temporary, that the protesters will soon take to the barricades again and the city will erupt once more.

Little wonder, then, that Eaton quickly gets smacked around like a piñata on his Twitter feed by Orioles fans.

Exactly twelve minutes later he's forced to issue a statement that reads like a jab at the humor-impaired and a mangled apology all in one.

"Take it easy, people," he tweets in response. "Just trying to lighten the mood. I have the utmost respect for Baltimore and its people. Always have, always will."

Batting practice gives the players from both teams their first taste of the bizarre setting that awaits them: the THWOCK! of Louisville Slugger meeting ball sounds like a cannon blast amid the empty seats, even over the rumble of military vehicles outside the ballpark and the classic rock tunes playing over the sound system.

Now that he's feeling contrite and has put his phone away

and turned his thoughts to baseball once more, Eaton voices another concern: how different will it be to track batted balls in the outfield?

With the crack of the bat now so exaggerated in the stillness, will outfielders automatically break a few steps back only to see catchable balls drop in front of them for base hits?

If the ball gets by the catcher with a runner on first, without the roar of the crowd will outfielders know something's happened and that they need to back up second in case the runner goes?

Caleb Joseph, on the other hand, has something more mundane on his mind: will the national anthem be played with no one in the ballpark? And why should it be? Why would tradition be upheld and a two-hundred-year-old ode to the flag be sung by the usual smiling local artist or a cappella group when there's no one in the stands to hear it?

Actually details are starting to trickle in about what will and won't be missing from this bizarre game.

Yes, "The Star-Spangled Banner" will played. But instead of being sung as usual by a live performer it'll be a canned instrumental version for the first time in recent memory.

Yes, there will be the usual personalized walk-up music. God forbid Orioles right fielder Delmon Young strolls to the plate without Wiz Khalifa's inspiring "We Dem Boys" blaring. And how could the bullpen doors swing open and Zach Britton be expected to close out another win without AC/DC's adrenaline-whipping "For Those About to Rock" blasting his eardrums?

And, yes, the usual seventh-inning stretch song will play. As always this will be John Denver's "Thank God I'm a Country Boy," the tune the singer famously belted out atop the Orioles' dugout during Game One of the 1983 World Series against the Philadelphia Phillies at now-demolished Memorial Stadium.

But, predictably, lots of the scoreboard touches so integral to the fan experience—for better or worse—will be missing.

There will be no Kiss Cam, for which couples react with feigned astonishment and smooch awkwardly when their images flash on the video screen. No goofy condiment races between mustard, ketchup, and relish as they circle the bases atop cartoon hotdogs that look as if they've languished for hours under warming lights at a 7-Eleven.

No "Crab Shuffle," in which fans try to follow swirling cartoon crabs to guess which one is hiding the baseball. No "Guess the Year" quiz centered on a memorable Orioles highlight from the past.

Instead the only thing shown between innings on the scoreboard will be the smiling visage of the Oriole Bird.

How long can you look at that? Caleb Joseph wonders. *And is that going to get anyone going?*

Ballplayers, he knows, use all the scoreboard silliness for entertainment between innings much as fans do. Now, without it, they might have to actually—gulp—focus on baseball the whole time.

On the other hand Gordon Beckham, Chicago's reserve infielder, reveals a hitherto unknown tactic he says the White Sox might employ to amuse themselves: silent clapping in the dugout.

Silent clapping?

Like when a teammate gets a hit or makes a great play in the field, he means. To demonstrate, he pantomimes a clap with both palms coming close to each other but ultimately touching only air.

"To kind of add to the ambience," he explains.

Or lack of same, as the case may be.

Outside the ballpark Lt. Dennis Reinhard, the BPD's stadium commander, is dealing with an unexpected issue of his own as the start of the game approaches.

The BC parking lot just south of Camden Yards is the staging area for the National Guard, the Maryland State Police, and the police officers from dozens of other cities and municipalities who have rushed to Baltimore to help keep the peace.

The place is crawling with so many troops and so much weaponry that Reinhard has taken to calling it "Fort Camden."

Now dozens of off-duty police officers from the "Fort" are trickling over to Home Plate Plaza, the only open entrance, hoping to get in to see the game. As much as he hates playing the heavy, Reinhard must quickly disabuse them of that notion.

The Orioles have made it clear, he tells them: no one is allowed in the seating bowl.

No one.

Sorry.

"Appreciate all your help, love you to death, but you're not coming in," he tells them.

This, predictably, does not go over well with his uniformed brethren, who have visions of kicking back in a prime seat on this gorgeous day and maybe even getting a little suntan while seeing this one-of-a-kind sports spectacle up close and personal.

"Oh, come on, lieutenant!" they beg. "This is cool! We want to see this!"

Which forces Reinhard to lapse into his Hardass Cop mode: a gimlet-eyed stare and a chillingly quiet, "You're just not hearing me, are you?"

Only then do the disappointed police and soldiers, mopey faces firmly affixed to let the lieutenant know how much he's killing them, retreat back to their staging areas.

The fact is that there are only six BPD officers and Reinhard himself stationed at the ballpark today to provide security. And they're here mainly in case an overly enthusiastic fan, with half the contents of a brewery sloshing around in his gut, attempts to scale the fence and get a better look at his heroes.

But the Orioles' brass was emphatic that even these cops

were to keep out of sight. Which is why three of them are now patrolling where the fans have gathered outside the left-field gates, even though the gates look tall enough and sturdy enough to repel an invasion of Visigoths.

With time for the first pitch fast approaching Jim Hunter, the announcer for the Orioles' Mid-Atlantic Sports Network (MASN), signs off his pregame show by saying: "Well, enjoy the game! Because if you're watching this, it's the only way you'll be able to see it."

It's a truism that provokes a particular sadness in this most rabid of fan bases. And it's been a hot topic in sports-talk radio all day.

Caller after caller—Joe from Perry Hall, Adam in Dundalk, Wayne in Severna Park—sounds a similar lament: "The most unusual baseball game ever—history making!—and we can't get in to see it. Only in Baltimore!"

11

BASEBALL IS A SPORT that fiercely and unabashedly collates a mind-numbing array of statistics from the mundane to the essential.

For those who savor the ever-growing buffet of advanced metrics—OPS, WAR, WHIP, Babip, FIP, and the like—these are the best of times to be a fan. Because numbers are so entwined with the history of the game, goes the argument, these new measurements paint a vivid portrait of a player's and team's strengths and weaknesses as never before.

For others the total effect is eye glazing. As are the dubious "records" baseball constantly trots out: first player to hit fifty doubles with 150 walks, only catcher over age thirty-five to hit twenty-five homers, etc.

Nevertheless, in the frantic hours since the decision was made to play the White Sox with no fans in attendance, the

Orioles' PR staff has been scrambling to quantify just how unusual this game will be.

What they come up with is this: there's never been anything even remotely like it.

According to the ubergeeks at the Society for American Baseball Research (SABR), Major League Baseball's previous low attendance was recorded 133 years ago, in September 1882 to be precise.

That was when the Troy (NY) Trojans played the Worcester Ruby Legs in Worcester, Massachusetts, in front of a crowd—if that's even the right word—of six. The Ruby Legs disbanded the following season, possibly due, some said, to being saddled with such a hideous nickname.

A wacky promotional stunt called "Nobody Night," put on by the Charleston Riverdogs, a Class A affiliate of the Tampa Bay Devil Rays, is credited for setting the previous record low for all of professional baseball.

On that hot July night in 2008 the gates to Joseph P. Riley Jr. Park in Charleston, South Carolina, were padlocked, and only players, employees, scouts, and media were allowed in to see the Riverdogs play the Columbus (OH) Red Stixx.

Fans who were turned away were urged to kill time by attending a party with discounted food and beer outside the ballpark. They were then allowed back in after the fifth inning, when the game was declared official and the attendance duly noted as zero.

The Riverdogs ended up losing 4–2. But from all accounts nobody seemed to care all that much, possibly because of the copious amounts of cheap beer that had been consumed.

No one seemed surprised that the team would pull such a stunt either. After all the 'Dogs were owned by Mike Veeck, whose father, St. Louis Browns owner Bill Veeck, had once sent a midget—wearing uniform number 1/8—to the plate in order to coax a walk in a 1951 game against the Detroit Tigers.

In the spirit of such bizarre maneuvers the younger Veeck

had also dreamed up events such as "Vasectomy Night," which was cancelled at the last minute when a local church, Veeck noted, got "snippy."

Another beauty was "Tonya Harding Bat Day," which served to attract both national media attention, editorials decrying the crassness of such an event, and plenty of spectators willing to pay cold, hard cash to be on hand.

Then there was "Labor Day," when pregnant women got in for free. And "Mullet Day," when history's worst haircut was proudly displayed by a succession of men seemingly unaware that the look had not been in favor for many, many years.

"Stay classy, Charleston," some critics would mutter about these Veeck-inspired stunts, shaking their heads sadly.

But Veeck never gave a fig about what his detractors thought.

"Fun is good" was his motto. And if that fun came in the form of a hilariously snarky promotion like "Lawyers Night," in which all lawyers were charged double to get in, then so be it.

As far as Major League attendance figures are concerned, during the first game of a doubleheader between the Florida Marlins and Cincinnati Reds in the summer of 2011, with Hurricane Irene bearing down on Miami, 347 fans were in the stands for the first pitch.

But with the Marlins counting tickets sold, not actual butts in the seats, the final attendance figure was listed—laughably—at over twenty-two thousand.

(Ironically the previous attendance low for a game in Baltimore, at old Memorial Stadium on Thirty-Third Street, also came against the White Sox. This was a makeup game played in August 1972 before just 655 fans. Making it even more embarrassing: the Orioles were in first place at the time.)

But as baseball statisticians are pointing out, postponements of Major League games for reasons not weather related—such as the ones here Monday and Tuesday—are rare but not unprecedented.

The start of the 1968 season, for example, was pushed back following the assassination of Rev. Martin Luther King, when black players led by Roberto Clemente and Bob Gibson refused to play until after King's funeral.

The SABR folks also report that after the notorious Rodney King verdict in 1992, the Los Angeles Dodgers postponed their four home games against Montreal due to rioting that engulfed the city for five days.

Six years later, a five-hundred-pound concrete and steel beam worked loose from the upper deck of Yankee Stadium and crashed into the empty stands below three hours before the Yankees were to play the Anaheim Angels.

The stadium was quickly closed for repairs; two games of the series were postponed. The third was moved to nearby Shea Stadium, home of the New York Mets.

And when the Loma Prieta earthquake shook the Bay Area during the 1989 World Series between the Oakland Athletics and San Francisco Giants, collapsing highways and engulfing the Mission District in fires, the games were postponed for a week and a half.

The horrific September 11 terrorist attacks in New York and Washington caused commissioner Bud Selig to delay all games on the schedule for a full week. And the Boston Red Sox cancelled a game in April 2013 when police were scouring the city for the Boston Marathon bombers who had killed 3 people and wounded 180 others.

All those postponed games were eventually made up in front of fans, however. But the SABR people claim that today's Orioles–White Sox contest marks the first time that *any* of the four major sports—baseball, football, basketball, and hockey—has intentionally been played without fans.

One of their members, Northwestern University professor Bill Savage, goes so far as to say MLB officials are making a big mistake by playing the game behind locked gates.

The optics, he says, are horrible.

Especially in this age when perception—more than ever—is reality.

"If it's not safe for fans to come to the game," Savage tells wired.com, "but it's safe for the players, that reinforces the fact that fans and players live in different universes."

Of course a comparison of fan/player paychecks alone would reinforce that perception to any sentient human being.

But Savage's point is that, by playing behind locked gates just hours after a devastating riot, baseball appears greedy and tin-eared, willing to do anything to keep at least part of its economic engine revving.

"Everyone else in town might have to shut down," he continues, "but they're going to bus in fifty ballplayers, ten coaches, four umpires and some clubhouse guys and play a ballgame in an empty stadium to fulfill contractual obligations to television."

Those obligations are not insignificant in terms of the club's financial health, though.

According to the *Sport Business Journal* the Orioles have the fifth-highest TV ratings of all twenty-nine U.S.-based Major League teams. The game will be broadcast in the Baltimore region by MASN and in major market Chicago by WPWR.

It's also being offered as MLB.com's free game of the day, ensuring it'll be seen by hundreds of thousands of viewers around the country. And of course the game will be heard on radio in both markets.

There are other numbers in play as the Orioles and White Sox prepare to square off in sleepy Camden Yards.

Even though owner Peter Angelos has made it clear that the team's focus is on the plight of the city and those who are suffering versus its own bottom line, the Orioles already know they're about to take a financial hit.

They've been averaging a little over thirty-three thousand fans per game this season. Which means they stand to lose millions of dollars in concession revenue, parking, and ticket sales for this game and the next three "home" contests in Tampa.

(It's hard to be more precise on the lost money; a team spokesman will make it clear that the Orioles never comment on their business-related finances.)

Yet this is a team that *Forbes* says is worth around $1 billion, and one that generated some $245 million in revenue in 2014. And while there is no way of knowing for sure at the moment, the club may be eligible for economic relief from MLB's Central Fund due to the unique circumstances of the postponed games.

Whatever the eventual economic impact this much is clear: no other team in baseball would want to trade places with the Orioles right now.

Instead twenty-eight other teams will be looking on with something approaching morbid curiosity. The setting could not be more incongruous: baseball, our most peaceful and pastoral sport, in a city that feels like an armed camp.

12

FOR ADAM JONES IT'S finally showtime.

Wearing a black warm-up jersey and bathed in white-hot TV lights, he sits in front of a single microphone at a table in the auxiliary clubhouse, which the Orioles use for pre- and postgame news conferences.

Around him dozens of digital recorders lie scattered like colorful seashells, already whirring silently to preserve his words for posterity—or at least until the next deadline.

It's a packed house, all right. Gazing up at him expectantly are row after row of reporters seated on metal chairs, with the overflow crowd lined up along the back behind the wall of television cameras.

None of this is terribly comforting to the Orioles' center

fielder, who, even as he leans toward the mic, is *still* trying to piece together what he plans to say.

One of these times, he thinks, *I should write this shit down.*

But it's too late for that now.

Besides, that wouldn't be Adam Jones. Scripting something is definitely not his style. He's been a high-wire act in any interview he's ever given, generally choosing his words carefully but always working without a metaphorical net.

If he falls and goes splat and says something dumb, so be it.

But he doesn't fall often.

This is a man who has always prided himself in speaking from the heart, if not the head, on all sorts of topics. In his eighth season with the Orioles he's earned tremendous respect with his teammates and the local media for being a straight shooter who never shies from addressing even the most controversial topics.

As he mentally prepares his remarks he's bent on striking a measured tone: empathy for the plight of the protesters, disavowal of the looting and burning, respect for the police and National Guard soldiers putting their lives on the line to protect the city.

That last point is important to him. His dad was ex-military and Jones grew up with law enforcement folks in his community; a great friend of his beloved "Moms" was a police officer.

So this will be another challenging session with the media, fraught with potential for misunderstanding as he tries to explain what he feels inside about the pain of so many in his adopted hometown.

In a sense, though, he's been rehearsing for this moment since the Freddie Gray protests first turned violent Saturday night.

That was when Zach Britton, Chris Davis, and other teammates began stopping by his locker and asking: "Jonesy, what do you think about all the stuff that's happening?"

The truth is that Jones sees a kindred spirit in both the

hard-throwing lefty closer and the slugging first baseman. *They get it,* Jones thinks. *They get what poverty and social injustice can do to people.*

They get it, he knows, because of their backgrounds.

Britton was born and raised in California before the family moved to the small northeast Texas town of Weatherford (population twenty-eight thousand). His mother, Martha Rosamaria Britton, grew up dirt poor in the Dominican Republic before making her way to the down-on-its-heels California town of Hawthorne, just a long home run from notorious, gang-infested Compton.

When he first met her, Zach's father was amazed to discover that his future bride had just one pair of shoes to her name. Hearing stories of his mother's tough upbringing made Britton acutely attuned at an early age to the plight of the less fortunate.

One of the things he loved most about pro baseball was the diversity he saw in the clubhouse—players from different countries, players from different socioeconomic backgrounds—at every stop on his way to the Major Leagues.

Over and over again he marveled at the incredible challenges some of his teammates had to overcome just to have food in their bellies and clothes on their backs, never mind to pursue a career in the game they loved.

Davis grew up in humble circumstances in Longview, Texas, a town of about seventy thousand people. His father worked for a company that did maintenance for railroad cars. But the elder Davis was often laid off for long periods and money was tight. At such times the family relied on the modest paychecks brought home by his mother, who was the financial secretary at their church.

Davis shared all this with Jones not long after he arrived in Baltimore in 2008, and the effect was instantaneous. The icy façade the cocky center fielder sometimes showed the world cracked. A bond developed between the two.

"Once he knew that about me, he was like, 'Okay,'" Davis says. "It kind of put our relationship at ease a little."

But Britton and Davis don't delude themselves. They know that no matter how difficult their lives were at times, they didn't have it nearly as tough as Jones did growing up in a bleak inner-city neighborhood.

"I'll never be able to understand how you feel," Davis has told Jones in the past. "What it feels like to be told to stay away from police officers—when you see one, run. I always thought: 'Okay, they're the good guys.'

"But that doesn't mean I can't appreciate what you go through and what you've been through. I need to be made aware of it. I need to be educated."

What Jones has been telling Britton and CD and every other Oriole who asks him about the tumult in the streets is this: "You gotta understand what these kids doing the protesting are going through. They're finally fed up with everything their parents and grandparents bitched and complained about—and rightfully so. Their parents and grandparents can't fight anymore. They're fighting for them.

"Try to put yourself in the shoes of the people that are hurting right now. Not just the people rioting, not just the store-owners who lost their livelihoods, but the police, too. We have an opportunity as a team to rally around the city and help a lot of people."

Sometimes, if the conversation gets heavy with one of his white teammates, Jones might get deeper into race and identity and what he is at his core, how it makes his life so different from theirs.

Because, see, he *wants* them to know why it's different.

No, check that. He *needs* them to know why it's different.

"I play ball, yeah," he might tell them. "But at the end of the day, I'm a black man. Strip away my money, take away everything else, I'm a black man. If I walk around the streets here in Baltimore and people see my face it's, 'Oh, there's

Adam Jones.' But strip away me playing baseball, I'm just a normal black dude.

"Especially when I go to another city, with the way I dress, comfortable sweats, long-sleeve shirt—I still get these looks. It sucks that that's how society is. But I understand it. It is what it is."

Hang with him someplace other than Baltimore, Jones tells people, and watch this uneasy interaction for yourself.

Watch what happens when he gets on the elevator in one of the upscale hotels the Orioles stay at in New York or Boston or Chicago. Watch the white women give him that wary look and clutch their handbags closer to their chests.

On a few such occasions—joking but sort of *not* joking, too—he's even blurted out: "Lady, I don't want that ugly bag!" Just to see the stricken look that comes over them.

At other times he says nothing and this darkly humorous, Richard Pryor–like riff begins playing in his head:

Now if we were in some seedy motel, meaning we're both kind of down and out, I might want your damn bag! In fact, it might be: "Gimme your bag!"

But they hurt, these encounters with suspicious white people on elevators and sidewalks and in parking garages. When they see him and don't know he's Adam Jones, Baltimore Orioles superstar, fabulously wealthy, polite, even keeled, law abiding and blah, blah, blah.

No threat to you or your well-being, folks.

"The stereotype," he says, meaning Dangerous Black Man with Criminal Intent, "is the part that always sucks."

Yet now, in front of this big room packed with all these national reporters studying him like he's some kind of African American oracle ready to put the unrest and a hundred-plus years of socioeconomic injustice in perspective, he knows he has to confine his remarks to what's happening here in the streets.

The idea that this game they're about to play could help the city return to the "normalcy" alluded to by Eaton and other players rankles Adam Jones on a gut level. It's this very "normalcy"—at least when it comes to the unchanging conditions in the poorest black neighborhoods—that caused Baltimore to erupt in the first place.

But the truth is that Jones, as smart as he is, as engaged as he tries to be, is young and only dimly aware of his adopted city's painful past when it comes to race and poverty.

He's not up on the segregation that dated back to the early twentieth century, when an ordinance effectively divided the city into black blocks and white blocks.

Nor is he aware of a report—released this very day, ironically—by the Economic Policy Institute, a nonpartisan think tank, that claims "the distressed condition of African-American working and lower-middle-class families" in Baltimore "is almost entirely attributable to federal policy that prohibited black families from accumulating housing equity during the suburban boom that moved white families into single-family homes from the mid-1930s to the mid-1960s—and thus from bequeathing that wealth to their children and grandchildren, as white suburbanites have done."

There were other scourges in those distressed neighborhoods that Jones is also not schooled on: the explosion in the availability of cheap heroin in the seventies, the closing of the steel mills and shipyards that made so many much-needed blue-collar jobs disappear, the crack cocaine epidemic of the eighties, the homicidal gang wars of the nineties, and the unrelenting gun violence of the first decade of the twenty-first century—almost all of it confined to the city's poorest areas.

Finally the young center fielder hasn't seen a report from the *Sun* that says the city paid out nearly $6 million from 2011 to 2014 to Baltimoreans who had lodged abuse charges against the police—and $45 million for two incidents of "rough rides" in police vans that ended up with the people being arrested also being paralyzed.

Yet what Jones *does* know from doing so much community work in Baltimore's poor neighborhoods, where he works with the club's RBI (Reviving Baseball in Inner Cities) program among others, is this: the poverty, crime, drug addiction, and joblessness mirror what was all around him growing up in southeast San Diego.

In a 2012 *Baltimore Sun* article that appeared not long after he signed his whopping $85.5 million contract extension, Jones's childhood friend Quintin Berry—now an outfielder with the Chicago Cubs—recalled that seven of their friends in their old neighborhood died because of gang-related violence.

But as poor as Jones was the gang-bangers left him alone. They sensed that his athletic prowess would one day carry him far and allow him to escape his bleak surroundings.

A few years later it did: in 2003 he was selected in the first round of the MLB draft, the thirty-seventh pick overall, by the Seattle Mariners.

"Now when I see those guys," Jones said of his old homeboys, "they say, 'It's awesome that you made it. You're living everybody's dream.'"

He was blessed, he knows, with a fiercely devoted mother, Andrea Bradley, who raised him and his four brothers and sisters mostly by herself. And with the kind parents of friends who took him in during transient periods of his youth and helped him emotionally and financially, buying him Mizuno baseball gloves and paying his way to AAU tournaments when he could afford neither. And with mentors who looked out for him and encouraged him.

It's this kind of support system that so many in the toughest neighborhoods of West Baltimore lack. That's the "normalcy" in the city that must change to avoid this kind of unrest happening again.

Hell, Jones's father-in-law, Jean Fugett, still lives in West Baltimore. A former NFL tight end with the Dallas Cowboys and Washington Redskins who went on to become an accomplished lawyer, Fugett has plenty of stories about what that kind of "normalcy" can do to a community, how it can beat you down if you let it.

So when Jones finally speaks to this roomful of reporters it's with more than a hint of sadness in his voice. On his face you can read the worry he's been feeling for days.

"We need this game to be played," he says. "But we need this city to be healed first. That's what's important to me. Because this is an ongoing issue. I just hope the community of Baltimore stays strong, the children of Baltimore stay strong, get some guidance, and heed the message of the city leaders."

He goes on to talk about the tough time the city is going through, how so many people are hurting no matter what race they are.

He talks about how much damage the unrest has done, but also about how much good the peaceful protests have accomplished, young people sticking up for their rights and railing against a deck so clearly stacked against them.

Maybe halfway through his remarks his tone seems to shift.

Suddenly he seems to be simultaneously addressing both the young protesters in the streets and his mostly white, mostly middle-class media audience.

"I've said to the youth: your frustration is warranted. It's understandable," he says. "The actions I don't think are acceptable. But if you come from where they come from, you understand.

"But I just think that ruining the community you have to live in is never the answer, due to the fact that you're going to have to wake up in three or four days and just go right back to those convenience stores, go right back to all those stores."

There is a pause here, a slight shrug of the shoulders, as if maybe he sees part of himself—his young self growing up, anyway—in the faces of the angry, disillusioned activists behind the nation's latest fiery upheaval.

"I think that this is their cry," he continues. "Obviously it's a cry that isn't acceptable. But this is their cry. And therefore we have to understand it. Like I said, they need hugs, they need love, they need support. I'm gonna try to give as much as I can. Because the city needs it."

Moments later Jones pushes away from the microphone and heads back to the clubhouse. The bright lights snap off and the reporters head back to their laptops to file their stories, their fresh Adam Jones quotes at the ready.

His message of empathy and solidarity will soon be up on websites and TV news reports all over the country. It will play especially well in the hardscrabble African American neighborhoods of Baltimore.

And the local and national media will eat it up.

"Adam always wanted to be the leader of this club since the time he first arrived here," MASN reporter Roch Kubatko will say later. "And the veterans would look at him like: 'Kid, your time will come. It's just not right now.'

"And even though you gradually saw it as the years went by, just by example, the way he played every day and being as vocal as he was, I don't think he ever exuded his leadership to the degree that he did [today]."

But in this traumatized city, where long-standing divisions of race and class have again been laid bare, not everyone will embrace Adam Jones's remarks.

Instead many agree with President Barack Obama's statement, issued the day before in the White House Rose Garden, that the small group of protesters who rioted "took advantage of the situation for their own purposes" and should be "treated as criminals."

Jones understands how even the most racially enlightened citizens might be uncomfortable expressing compassion for those who looted and destroyed—no matter how dire the living conditions that prompted it.

But desperation has led to violence since the dawn of humanity.

What was it the great Martin Luther King said? "A riot is the voice of the unheard"?

Yes, that's it exactly.

Most of the time, Adam Jones thinks, *you have to make people uncomfortable before real systemic change can occur.*

As he stands in front of his locker now, getting ready to play a baseball game that has never seemed so inconsequential, he wonders if what he just said to the roomful of national media will make anyone uncomfortable at all.

Probably not, is the verdict.

Might have to try a little harder next time.

13

A HALF HOUR BEFORE game time Caleb Joseph is the first Oriole clambering through the dugout to take the field. But instead of heading directly to the bullpen to warm up today's starter, his usual routine, the catcher makes a curious move.

He veers left and faces the empty stands.

Now he pretends to sign autographs and high-five grateful fans, all the while carrying on a make-believe conversation complete with nods, chuckles, and a thumbs-up sign, seemingly thanking them for their support.

After a moment or two he doffs his cap, shoots an index finger triumphantly toward the sky, and trots toward the bullpen, catcher's mask and chest protector cradled in one arm.

From all outward appearances he has gone absolutely bonkers.

But this whole peculiar kabuki is not over just yet.

In the middle of the outfield he suddenly stops, turns toward the stands, and executes a sweeping operatic bow, drinking in the nonexistent cheers from the crowd that isn't there.

After a final series of waves toward the adoring masses in

all parts of the ballpark—*YES! YES! I LOVE YOU TOO!*—he disappears behind the blue outfield wall and into the bull-pen. At last he might be ready to warm up Ubaldo Jimenez, who will be taking the mound for the Orioles.

Hoo boy.

Although it might appear to the uninitiated that Joseph is having some sort of psychotic episode, it's just Caleb being Caleb. At least that's what the Orioles will say when they discover the little show their free-spirited catcher has put on for the benefit of 45,971 empty seats and random TV cameras that have captured the whole thing.

The guy's just having some fun, his teammates say. And whatever that crazy act of his was, it helped drain some of the tension that's been building steadily in this place as the afternoon wears on.

"Normally, before a game, there's a huge bunch of kids yelling and screaming for your autograph right next to the dugout," Joseph will explain later with a soft smile. "I've never been able to stop and sign for them, 'cause I feel like there's so many and I have to go begin my workday and don't want to leave anyone out. Today I stopped."

Ohhh-kay . . .

Whether that explanation does or doesn't make any sense—and many will lean toward the latter—it was another example of Caleb Joseph wringing every ounce of joy that he can from his improbable journey to "the Show."

A few years earlier he almost gave up on the game after being seemingly trapped forever in the baseball purgatory that is the Minor Leagues. He spent so much time with the Bowie Baysox, the Orioles' Double-A affiliate, that people took to calling him "the Mayor of Bowie"—never a good sign when your sights are set on the bright lights of Camden Yards.

Yet when Ubaldo Jimenez, the veteran right-hander, joins him in the bullpen, it's time for both men to forget Joseph's one-man farce and get serious.

At thirty-one Jimenez, a native of the Dominican Republic, is coming off a disappointing 2014 season. After signing a four-year, $50 million deal, the most lucrative contract ever given to a free-agent starter by the Orioles, he posted a 6-9 record and 4.81 ERA.

His hard-working, nice-guy demeanor has won over the veterans in the clubhouse. But Jimenez knows he has a lot more to prove to his teammates, his manager, and the Orioles' fan base, which is already getting restless with his slow start and taking shots at him on social media.

As Jimenez stretches Joseph studies his pitcher's face, looking for signs of nerves. But there are none. Tall and lanky, with boyish features and a ready grin, Jimenez appears to have the same placid demeanor that he always does.

Just before beginning his warm-up tosses he looks around the empty stadium and shakes his head in wonder.

"Wow," he says to his catcher, "this is kind of crazy!"

Who could argue with that assessment?

The last time Jimenez played in front of no fans was in the Dominican Summer League in 2001, when he was seventeen. As anyone who played there could testify, there was little danger of anyone, except maybe a couple of *borrachos*, showing up to watch rookie-level ball on a sun-parched field in the broiling heat and humidity of San Pedro de Macoris.

As soon as Jimenez begins loosening his arm it's as if a switch has been thrown somewhere in his cerebral cortex.

Suddenly his eyes narrow. His brow furrows. His expression turns serious.

Joseph watches all of this approvingly.

He's getting into the zone, the catcher thinks as the ball begins popping into his mitt with a louder and louder *WHAP!*

In the past Joseph has tried to explain the zone to casual baseball fans. But they don't always get it, especially the nonathletes.

The zone, he knows, is a heightened state of concentration that allows a pitcher to blot out the noise of sixty thousand fans—or the deafening silence of no fans—and focus solely on getting the batter out.

It allows him to play loose and free and without nerves as his tunnel vision zeroes in solely on his catcher and the target that's he's putting up sixty feet six inches away. And the truth is that, even though Jimenez knows it's magnified by their surroundings, the louder-than-normal sound of the ball slamming into Joseph's mitt is helping the pitcher's confidence as well.

Man, he tells himself, *that feels good! Might be a good day!*

As the Orioles and White Sox finish stretching and doing some light running in the outfield, the enormity of playing in this sterile atmosphere is beginning to sink in.

Players in both dugouts are talking in hushed, respectful tones, aware that even normally modulated conversation carries everywhere. The usual joking and light banter is missing. This feels more like the moments before a church service than anything else.

Both Buck Showalter and Chicago manager Robin Ventura wonder how their players will summon the energy to compete at a high level when the noise and color of the fans, the very lifeblood of the game, are missing.

Sure, a few dozen Orioles diehards have gathered behind the locked gates in left-center field. They peer through the wrought-iron fence like some kind of latter-day Knothole Gang and hold up encouraging signs and banners. But their cheers, echoing through the vast empty canyons of green seats, only seem to reinforce the sense of torpor and isolation.

The players can hear them, all right. But they're so far away that they might as well be cheering from Montana.

In keeping with the mood, up in the Orioles' TV booth veteran play-by-play announcer Gary Thorne looks and sounds almost funereal as MASN's broadcast begins.

"Circumstances all of us wish were different," he says in

his opening monologue. "Because of what has gone on here in Baltimore, the civil disruption outside and for the safety of individuals, this ballpark today is going to be empty.

"For the first time in Major League history, a ballgame—a regular season ballgame—will be played with no fans in attendance. We wish that were otherwise today. And as Adam Jones said, all of us [are] thinking of this great city and its chance to recover."

Turning to his broadcast partner, Hall of Famer Jim Palmer, Thorne adds: "This is one of those moments where you may make history, but you really wish you didn't have to do it."

Palmer, the three-time Cy Young Award winner and the greatest pitcher in Orioles history, seems equally subdued.

He's been in Baltimore as part of this franchise for fifty years now, after a nineteen-year career with the Orioles. And although he was in Florida rehabbing an arm injury in 1968 when Martin Luther King was killed and the city exploded in deadly rioting, the desperation he hears from Baltimore's most impoverished neighborhoods seems the same now as it did then.

In his twenty-second year as an analyst on Orioles broadcasts, he's as polished as ever in his opening remarks, agreeing with Thorne that maybe this game will bring some sense of normalcy to this broken city.

But off the air he's not nearly as sanguine. Too many, he says, are still hurting in Baltimore's most distressed neighborhoods.

"I've been here since 1965," he's been telling people. "What's changed? Not a whole lot."

He waves his hands in the air and shrugs.

"Dale Petroskey," he says, referring to the former president of the National Baseball Hall of Fame, "talks about the 'Ovarian Lottery.' If you're born in this country, it's the land of opportunity. But not for everybody."

In the open-air press box one level down it's standing room only, with ninety-two local and national reporters shoehorned into three narrow levels of work space. Here the mood seems almost anthropological, as if all those hunched before their laptops and filling out their scorecards are about to study a baffling human interaction never seen before.

The unspoken question on everyone's mind: *What in God's name will this whole thing be like?*

As the Orioles take the field the voice of Orioles PA announcer Ryan Wagner, sounding even more stentorian than usual, requests that the "ladies and gentlemen" in attendance rise for the national anthem.

And now, with the Orioles and White Sox standing at respectful attention in the field and in front of their dugouts, a canned version of "The Star-Spangled Banner" blares.

It is an absolutely gorgeous spring day. The sun is shining brightly. Large white, puffy clouds float in the cerulean sky.

If you close your eyes it almost feels as though you're at a normal baseball game.

But not when you open them again and take a long, hard look around.

14

THE FIRST PITCH IS officially recorded at 2:06 p.m. It's an eighty-seven-mile-per-hour fastball from Ubaldo Jimenez that the White Sox's leadoff batter, Adam Eaton, takes for strike one.

Even though this might be the fattest pitch he'll see all day the bat never moves off Eaton's shoulder. Given the somnambulant atmosphere it's fair to wonder if he hasn't dozed off for a second.

Before stepping into the batter's box Eaton had assumed that the natural rhythm of the game and the competitive juices of the players would provide enough sizzle to compensate for the lack of fan noise.

But now he sees how wrong he was.

Now he realizes how much he and his teammates feed off a big crowd—whether it's pulling for you or calling for you, your mother, your entire family plus your dog, to die in the most horrible, painful way.

He steps out, smooths the dirt in the box, and taps both cleats with his bat. He shakes his head almost imperceptibly and chomps furiously on his gum, seemingly trying to refocus.

"And this history-making ballgame is now officially in the books as having begun," Gary Thorne declares.

To Caleb Joseph, squatting behind the plate, the lack of reaction to the pitch by all parties in this hermetic ballpark is almost comical.

What planet are we on? he wonders. *At any normal game, the crowd would erupt in wild cheering for the first strike. It's practically the law . . .*

Not only was there zero response to that pitch, Joseph thinks, but the "Strike!" call by home-plate umpire Jerry Layne felt all wrong, too.

Layne, the crew chief and a twenty-six-year veteran, is not the most animated ump under the best of circumstances, Joseph knows.

But on that pitch, instead of signaling a strike in his usual manner with an emphatic pump of his right hand, Layne jabbed weakly with his index finger like a man pointing to the pastrami he wants at the deli counter.

His voice was so muted it almost sounded like a whisper.

"Jerry, don't be screaming in my ear now," Joseph says drily.

Layne cracks up. The deadpan remark is a good icebreaker for both men. The veteran ump, normally low-key and unflappable, is feeling as unsettled as everyone else in this weird new environment.

Eaton goes down swinging moments later on a nasty changeup by Jimenez that flutters and drops at the last second for strike three. And after Melky Cabrera bounces out to the pitcher and budding superstar Jose Abreu strikes out looking to end the inning, Jimenez walks off the mound with something almost resembling a strut.

Watching him return to the dugout, Showalter has to smile. *That's a good omen*, he thinks. *Good body language.*

Jimenez's fragile ego, Showalter knows, has taken a pounding with each successive bad outing in an Orioles uniform. The big contract, with the outsized expectations it engenders in the fan base, has been weighing on him—everyone on the team can see that.

He should do well today without anybody getting on him from the stands, Showalter thinks.

Some pitchers can handle that kind of abuse. Rolls right off their shoulders. But Ubaldo, as pleasant a human being as you could ever be around, is too thin-skinned for that. Heckling, to him, is almost an emotional form of waterboarding.

Jeff Samardzija, the tall, burly White Sox starter, does not fare nearly as well his first time through the Orioles' lineup.

A former two-time All-American wide receiver at Notre Dame who turned down the NFL for baseball, he's been texting back and forth with Chris Davis since the White Sox arrived in town.

The two know each other through a mutual friend, Chicago Cubs lefty reliever James Russell; both were in Russell's wedding party the previous off-season.

Samardzija has been picking Davis's brain about the unrest. With the White Sox holed up in the Hilton since Sunday night and hearing all sorts of wild rumors after Monday's violence in the streets, he's been trying to gauge the seriousness of the situation.

"SERIOUS," Davis responded to his buddy's first inquiry. "THIS IS FOR REAL."

Samardzija has something else weighing on his mind, too.

Four days earlier he'd played a leading role in an on-field brawl during Chicago's 3–2, thirteen-inning loss to the Kansas City Royals. It was the usual baseball fight: a few wild punches thrown to little effect, a lot of pushing and shoving and cursing, most of it involving various colorful permutations of "chickenshit" and "motherfucker."

Nevertheless, along with his teammate Chris Sale, Samardzija had been slapped with a five-game suspension, which he has been appealing.

But shortly after the Tuesday announcement that the Orioles and White Sox would be playing Wednesday's game in a locked-down stadium, he'd also learned he'd been tapped as Chicago's starting pitcher.

He texted the news to Davis, who proceeded to dust off the same weak line that would lead to a social-media smackdown for Adam Eaton.

"Guess you don't have to worry about taking our fans out of the game," Davis replied.

Samardzija got a grin out of that. But he seemed to quickly grow pensive.

"Honestly," he shot back, "I don't know what I'm gonna think or feel when the game starts."

"Dude," Davis replied, "you're not alone."

Whether it's the suspension he's facing, the sight of armed soldiers in the streets and police choppers overhead, or the eerie ballpark atmosphere, Samardzija is clearly off his game when he takes the mound.

The Orioles are only too happy to take advantage.

Before drawing a leadoff walk Alejandro De Aza fouls four pitches into the left-field stands, prompting Gary Thorne to remark: "Someone brought this up today. Could a player jump over the wall and go in the stands and try to make a catch?"

Thorne knows the answer, of course. But he's teeing one up for his broadcast partner, and also hoping to enlighten any fans not up on the rules.

"There's not going to be any fan interference, obviously," Palmer says.

But no, you can't do that, both men agree.

Jimmy Paredes hits a bouncer to first base that Abreu fields cleanly, but his throw to second for the force pulls shortstop Alexei Ramirez off the bag. And when Delmon Young follows with a bloop single to shallow center the bases are loaded.

Adam Jones drives in the game's first run with a sacrifice fly to right. And when Paredes tags up on the play and takes third, Orioles communications and marketing boss Greg Bader, watching from an open radio booth high above the field, hears two things he's never heard before in all his years in baseball.

First he hears the dirt spraying into the air as Paredes's spikes rake the basepath on his slide.

Then he hears the hollow thump of Paredes's foot striking the bag.

Both sounds are so clear it's almost as if the base had been miked for one of those gauzy baseball documentary scenes where the runner and ball race each other in super-slo-mo across the screen before—WHAP!–the ball slams into a fielder's outstretched glove for the tag and an out or—THUNK!—the runner's foot hits the base in a cloud of dust and the umpire cries, "SAFE!"

Samardzija's day gets even worse moments later. Into the batter's box steps his pal Chris Davis, who's been on a tear lately with four homers and thirteen runs batted in on the young season.

The slugging first baseman is a frightening sight for any pitcher: biceps rippling under his crisp, white uniform, two-day growth of scruffy beard, thick wad of tobacco bulging from one side of his mouth, a slash of eye-black on each cheekbone shining like war paint.

He holds the bat high and waves it menacingly in tiny circles as he calmly awaits the first pitch. Samardzija, peering in for the sign from catcher Geovany Soto, knows he can't afford to make a mistake here.

The season is barely a month old and Davis, a notoriously

streaky hitter, is starting to punish the ball no matter where it's thrown.

Davis fouls off a fastball and watches a slider break low and inside for a ball.

Then it happens.

Samardzija blunders badly and leaves an eighty-four-miles-per-hour changeup high in the zone. Davis's eyes widen. In an instant, he reaches out and flicks the bat, launching a bomb that curls just inside the right-field foul pole for a three-run homer and a 4–0 Orioles lead.

Thorne's call is a classic of the genre, excited and elliptical at the same time: "1-1 delivery . . . and he got a hold of that one! Will it stay fair . . . GOOD-BYE, HOME RUN!"

Both the crack of the bat and Thorne's animated commentary reverberate around the deserted ballpark. And as he begins his home-run trot Davis marvels that this is the first time he's actually heard a Major League announcer call one of his shots in real time.

As he circles the bases he hears the muffled cheers of the two dozen fans peering through the gates beyond left field. He also picks up the celebration in the Orioles' dugout, and the sounds are so clear and honest—like back in Little League—that it almost moves him to tears.

This is awesome! he thinks on his jog. *Thank you, God!*

But the stoic look on his face never changes and he keeps his head down even as he crosses home plate. Only when he slaps hands with Young and Manny Machado and bangs forearms with Everth Cabrera and Jonathan Schoop does he permit himself a small smile.

Not once does he look at his buddy, Samardzija, even as he works his way through the dugout gauntlet of high-fiving teammates showering him with sunflower seeds. Which is just as well because the big righty appears to be staring into space, seemingly shocked at how quickly the game has gotten away from him.

It only gets worse when Machado doubles to center and the next batter, Cabrera, drives the Orioles' third baseman home with another double down the left-field line.

White Sox pitching coach Don Cooper quickly visits the mound in an attempt to settle down his pitcher. But this is akin to giving a pep talk to a coal miner after the mine shaft has caved in around him.

It doesn't work anyway. Moments later Caleb Joseph's bloop single over the head of second baseman Micah Johnson drives in yet another run to make it 6–0 Orioles.

"And Jeff Samardzija's wondering what is going on!" Jim Palmer says in the understatement of the day.

Rey Navarro makes the second out of the inning when he lifts a foul ball down the right-field line and Avisail Garcia makes a terrific sliding catch.

But De Aza, batting for the second time in the inning, prolongs Samardzija's torture with a slow bouncer up the middle for a base hit. Sensing the possibility of a catastrophic meltdown by their starter, the White Sox quickly have righty Scott Carroll up and warming in the bullpen.

But Jimmy Paredes is retired on a grounder to second, and as he walks off the mound a shaken Samardzija is practically mumbling to himself.

If he bothers to look up he can see a medical chopper headed to a nearby Shock Trauma center, a fitting backdrop for one of the ugliest innings of his big-league career.

When the Orioles take the field and Caleb Joseph begins warming up Jimenez for the start of the second inning, Joseph hears an announcement in the press box: "Chris Davis's home run was the eightieth in the history of Camden Yards to land on Eutaw Street."

Wow, that's interesting, Joseph thinks. *When would you ever hear something like that over the crowd noise at a normal game?*

Not that a normal game wouldn't look pretty good about now.

15

BOB DAVIDSON HAS NEVER seen anything like the bizarre drama unfolding here as the game goes on.

And Davidson knows bizarre. He's seen a ton of it in his baseball life.

A Major League umpire for twenty-five years, he's still infamous in certain circles for ejecting the Montreal Expos mascot Youppi! from a home game against the Los Angeles Dodgers in 1989, an incident that will grace his Wikipedia listing from now to eternity.

Who tosses a cute, furry mascot out of a game? No one had ever done it before. But that didn't stop Davidson.

When the excitable Youppi!, inexplicably clad in a nightgown and old-fashioned nightcap and carrying a pillow, began jumping with gusto atop the Dodgers' dugout before plopping down in a front-row seat, Tommy Lasorda quickly got the red ass.

The crusty skipper complained to the umps in his usual way—loudly and profanely. It fell to Davidson at third base to rectify the situation. Clearly Youppi! had to go. So Davidson gave him the thumb as a chorus of boos rained down from the Olympic Stadium fans.

Lasorda, bless him, stayed in character throughout too.

As security removed the chastened mascot—luckily his furry orange arms were too big for handcuffs—the Dodgers' manager serenaded him with a stream of epithets that made the little old ladies in the first row blanch and clutch their pearls.

You want bizarre?

That was bizarre, Davidson will tell you.

Having "mean, heartless ump who ran Youppi!" on your resume forever is a singular achievement not many can match.

Although for pure sustained weirdness, even the Youppi!

Affair can't top what he's witnessing here: a Major League game that feels as though it's being held in some sort of aseptic baseball biosphere to which the rest of the world has been denied access.

Ironically, in addition to a familiarity with out-of-control mascots, Davidson also turns out to have experience with riot-torn cities.

In late April of 1992 he was scheduled to work a three-game Dodgers-Expos series in LA. But hours earlier a jury had acquitted four police officers of using excessive force in the beating of an African American motorist named Rodney King, an incident that was captured on video and that stunned the entire nation.

The city exploded in six days of violence that left fifty-five dead, thousands injured, and over one billion dollars in damage. With dense smoke from hundreds of fires blanketing the city and reports of news helicopters and planes at the Los Angeles airport being shot at by gun-toting rioters, Davidson and his fellow umpires holed up at the Holiday Inn in Hollywood until the games were eventually postponed.

Now here he is, working second base in what could charitably be likened to an Arizona Instructional League atmosphere, but only if you could imagine cities like Tempe, Mesa, and Scottsdale under martial law and girding for an invasion by, say, Mexico.

The other umps kid Davidson that he's bad juju, that his mere presence has now caused an unprecedented civic conflagration in two different cities. But the gravity of the situation in Baltimore, they know, is no joking matter.

Davidson and his fellow umps have been in town since Sunday after taking the train down from New York, where they served over the weekend as the instant-replay crew at the Replay Command Center in Manhattan.

When the Baltimore riots started Monday and the game was postponed, they quickly heeded the advice of MLB security, which urged them not to stay at their usual Inner Harbor hotel. Instead they've been ensconced for the past two days at a hotel out near BWI Marshall Airport, watching with concern as the city appeared to be coming apart at the seams.

Davidson's wife, Denise, has flown in from their home in Colorado. Her sister, Carol Brubaker, has flown in from Des Moines. The two had planned to attend this game before taking a train up to New York to do some shopping.

But with the Orioles and the police strictly enforcing the empty-stadium policy, the two women have been exiled instead to a nearby restaurant, where Davidson hopes they'll be safe until the game is over.

All of this has the normally gregarious Davidson in a pensive mood, treading lightly in his usual banter with the players and coaches from both teams.

"Better be careful what you yell in the dugout, 'cause I'll be able to hear it," he jokingly warns Robin Ventura at one point. But much of his interaction with others on the field feels strained.

Davidson spent two years umpiring winter ball in the Dominican Republic and normally has an easy rapport with the Hispanic players. He addresses them as *feo*, which means "ugly" in Spanish.

They think that's funny. Knee-slapping hilarious, even. And they're constantly shooting the same good-natured put-down back at him.

Yet today, as he exchanges pleasantries with Jose Abreu and Alexei Ramirez of the White Sox and Manny Machado, the Orioles' budding superstar, Davidson senses the players aren't in the mood for any *feo* frivolity.

There's a businesslike air to both teams. And particularly for the White Sox, there's a vibe that translates to: "Let's get this over with and get out of Dodge."

Sitting in the dugout, Adam Jones knows one thing: there

1. Freddie Gray protestors and bar patrons clash Saturday evening, April 25, near Camden Yards prior to the Orioles–Red Sox game. AP Photo/Patrick Semansky.

2. Demonstrators mass outside Camden Yards in the hours before the Orioles take the field against the Red Sox. AP Photo/Patrick Semansky.

3. (*opposite top*) Protestors smash the windshield of a
police cruiser Saturday evening as violence breaks out near
Baltimore's Inner Harbor. Jim Watson/AFP/Getty Images.

4. (*opposite bottom*) Scoreboard message flashed in the
latter innings of the Orioles–Red Sox game warning fans
to remain inside as demonstrations continue outside the
ballpark. Patrick McDermott/Getty Images.

5. (*above*) Mourners file past Freddie Gray's casket at
his funeral on Monday, April 27, at New Shiloh Baptist
Church in West Baltimore. AP Photo/Patrick Semansky.

6. A lone cyclist watches a police cruiser burn in the hours after the Freddie Gray protests turned violent. Algerina Perna/*Baltimore Sun* via AP.

7. Looters descend on the CVS store at the corner of Pennsylvania and North Avenues as the rioting worsens. Images of dark smoke billowing from the burning store would serve as the defining image of a city devolving into chaos. WJLA via AP.

8. Against a dramatic backdrop of empty seats, Orioles slugger Chris Davis blasts a three-run homer in the first inning of Baltimore's eventual 8–2 win over the Chicago White Sox on Wednesday, April 29. Greg Fiume/Getty Images.

9. Orioles fans and members of the news media gather outside the locked gates beyond left field at Camden Yards. AP Photo/Matt Rourke.

10. Spectators watch the fanless game from room balconies and the fourth-floor courtyard of the Hilton hotel across the street from the ballpark. AP Photo/Gail Burton.

will be no real getting on the umps today. Even if Jerry Layne's strike zone is the size of a GMC Yukon.

If you say, "C'mon, that's a ball!" in a regular voice, they'll hear you, he thinks. *And if you really get hot and shout, "Hey, man, that was a horseshit call!" you better follow it with, "Yeah, that was me! Six!" Give him the uniform number of one of your teammates. Let them run THAT guy and not you . . .*

After the interminable first inning, when Samardzija suffers the pitcher's equivalent of death by a thousand paper cuts, the game progresses at a brisker pace.

The Orioles push another run across in the third inning on an RBI single by Caleb Joseph to go up 7–0. In this torpid atmosphere it's hard to believe the White Sox will be able to generate enough energy to make a comeback.

The more likely possibility, some feel, is that they mail it in the rest of the way and blow out as quickly as possible for the airport and their flight to Minnesota for another series with the Twins.

Nevertheless, whether the game zips by or drags on for hours, the umpires have the same job to do, and that's to focus and get the calls right.

As the early innings go by and the silence in the ballpark deepens, players on both teams seem to appreciate Layne's no-drama style and his use of his "indoor voice" behind the plate.

Man, Caleb Joseph thinks, *Jerry's the perfect guy to be calling balls and strikes in this one. An older veteran umpire is exactly what we need. There's no reason to be flamboyant. The people who need to know what he's saying are either sixty feet away from him or two and a half feet away. And they can hear everything.*

For first-base umpire Hunter Wendelstedt, a seventeen-year veteran, it has taken longer to get over the shock of a great American city imploding in violence and a ballgame forced behind locked gates.

Mostly this is because he has a much deeper connection to Baltimore than do Layne, Davidson, or third-base ump David Rackley. For one thing Wendelstedt's father, Harry Wendelstedt, a legendary National League umpire for thirty-two years, grew up in a large family in nearby Essex, Maryland.

Hunter Wendelstedt's own childhood was spent in Florida, and he now lives in Louisiana. But his family connection ensured that Hunter would have a lifelong affection for Baltimore, the blue-collar attitude of its people, and many of the city's quirky charms.

He especially developed a love over the years for its signature culinary delight: the Maryland crab cake.

Long ago his father passed down a deep appreciation for the hockey-puck-sized lump of jumbo crab meat, seasoned generously and browned to perfection, to the point where the younger Wendelstedt now considers himself a crab cake snob.

In fact, if there was anything good about waiting out the unrest in a nondescript hotel in the soulless suburban sprawl out by the airport, it was that it was near G&M Restaurant in Linthicum Heights, recognized by seafood aficionados as serving Maryland's absolute best crab cake.

Thus it was that, every day of their enforced idleness, Wendelstedt would drag his umpire buddies over to G&M for their meals. There they learned a valuable lesson: if you have to put up with mind-numbing Beltway traffic and the roar of planes taking off and landing at all hours, you might as well be tucking into a delicious crab cake platter and swilling a couple of cold beers.

Yet this visit to Camden Yards has been educational in a peculiar way.

When the umpires took the field for the first time an hour ago, Wendelstedt felt compelled to take cell phone videos of the emptiness all around him.

This is crazy! he thought. *Yet this is the beauty of baseball, too. When you think you've seen everything, there's always something else to see.*

Always something to learn too.

At one point between innings he wanders over to the tarp rolled up along the right-field line, where he's secreted a bottle of water. The ball girl stationed there approaches him hesitantly.

"Excuse me," she says, "is this weird for you?"

"It really is," Wendelstedt replies.

The ball girl nods and smiles softly.

Turns out, it's really weird for her, too.

For the very first time, she tells Wendelstedt, she's working a game without being besieged by fans begging her to toss them a ball she's retrieved.

For the first time people aren't pleading for a ball because it's their birthday. Or because it's their kid's first Major League game. Or because they say they have a fatal disease and they're about to leave this mortal coil and, boy, it sure would be great to go out clutching a piece of horsehide with Rawlings inscribed on it in their cold, dead fingers.

"I don't have to tell anyone 'no' today," she says, her smile getting wider.

Wendelstedt is stunned.

All these years in the Majors and he's never heard about the con games fans try to work on the ball girls, all the ridiculous lines they come up with just to walk away with something you can buy in any sporting goods store in the land for under ten bucks.

Man, he thinks, *you really do learn something new every day.*

As the game goes on, this lifeless exercise that *looks* like a baseball game but doesn't *feel* like one, he finds his thoughts drifting back to his late father. The two men, immensely proud of their shared profession, talked every day about baseball.

Harry Wendelstedt couldn't get enough of the game, even after a lifetime spent living and breathing it up close.

The day before he died in 2012 the elder Wendelstedt critiqued Hunter's work behind the plate in a meaningless spring training game televised on ESPN. And on the day he passed away the old man was actually watching a game on the MLB Network as they loaded him in an ambulance for his final ride to the hospital.

Wish I could tell him about this game, Wendelstedt thinks wistfully, looking around again. *Wouldn't that be great? To get his thoughts and feelings on all this stuff going on in his hometown?*

Then he shakes the thought from his head and goes back to doing his job, focusing once more on an exercise that feels more like a company softball game than anything else.

16

OUT BEYOND THE LEFT-FIELD wall, so far away they appear to be in another zip code, a loud contingent of Orioles fans is on hand.

That they would show up here in their orange and black gear, faces pressed through the wrought-iron railings to get even a few inches closer to the action, surprises absolutely no one who pays attention to this franchise.

For fourteen dreary seasons, from 1998 through 2011, Orioles fans were forced to watch some of the most horrid big-league baseball on the planet, played by some of the most inept teams imaginable, led by a succession of frustrated, overwhelmed, and, in many cases, spectacularly incompetent managers.

Those were the fourteen losing seasons that spawned talk of a legendary "Lost Generation of Orioles fans," which proved to be more myth than reality. Because still the fans came out. Maybe not in quite the same numbers as before. But there was no way that a majority of the base, as hard-core and devoted as any in the game, would turn its back on this team.

Yet not until after Buck Showalter—to many, the living incarnation of the sainted Earl Weaver, the best manager in franchise history—was hired in 2010 and Dan Duquette came aboard the following year did the losing stop. Then attendance at Camden Yards spiked even higher and the love affair between a city and its baseball team only deepened.

So they gather now behind the locked gates, peering past the bullpen picnic grove and the larger-than-life bronze sculptures of Orioles legends Brooks Robinson, Frank Robinson, Jim Palmer, Eddie Murray, Cal Ripken Jr., and the feisty Weaver.

The view isn't great. In fact it's actually pretty bad, narrow and distorted, as if the knot of fans has been struck with a collective case of macular degeneration. But that's not what this is about for these fans.

What this is about is an unwavering allegiance to a ballclub and the general mentality of Baltimore sports fans, who have a collective chip on their shoulder the size of a sequoia.

You won't open the gates and let us in? they seem to be saying. Too bad. We're showing up anyway. Sure, the whole country—hell, the whole the world—knows about the riots. And it's making the city look like crap again. But we'll be damned if it looks like nobody showed up to support our ballclub while all this was going on.

At the end of the first inning there are maybe four dozen spectators here; their numbers will swell and ebb as the game goes on.

Some were here for batting practice; many trickled in later. Following Baltimore tradition they yell, "O!" at the precise moment during the national anthem: "Oh, say does that star-spangled banner yet wave?"

You do that in this town because it's practically required

by statute. Because if you don't yell it at the top of your lungs you are no true fan of the Orioles and should probably be beaten with sticks.

"LET US IN!" someone cries now. But given all that has happened in this broken city over the past three days, it sounds more like a plaintive wail than a demand.

While the mood here is hopeful that the worst of the unrest might finally be over, it's hardly raucous, not with so much of the city still feeling like a war zone.

Not far away on Washington Boulevard, Sliders Bar & Grille, the Bullpen, and Pickles Pub are mostly deserted. Normally these bars would be teeming with baseball fans. But this was the scene of the wild bottle-throwing and fistfighting melee between demonstrators and fans four nights earlier; the Bullpen's shattered windows, in fact, are still boarded up.

No one's hanging out and swilling a few beers and talking about the O's. Instead, at the start of the game, there appeared to be exactly one customer outside all three of the popular saloons.

The sallow feel that hangs over the city extends to these fans behind the locked gates, despite their almost desperate attempts to shake it and cheer for their team.

One man holds a sign that says, "REMEMBER FREDDIE GRAY." Another, a fifty-three-year-old named Steve Orzol from Harford County, walks around with a poster depicting the Oriole Bird with a tear dripping from one eye.

Orzol says this is a sad day for Baltimore—*another* sad day, actually. He says he's tweeted to the mayor, urging her to open the gates.

"I told her she needs to do the right thing," Orzol tells the *Baltimore Sun*, echoing the thoughts of many here. "You have to let the fans in the game somehow. You have to talk to Major League Baseball, whatever, because you're staining Baltimore right now.

"You can do the right thing and we can look like a great

city," he continues. "If you open up these gates, show the country that it's not as bad as you think Baltimore is. What is this going to do to tourism?"

Tourism, however, is far from the thoughts of most Baltimoreans at the moment.

This is hardly the time for anyone to be strolling over to Harborplace for a cappuccino, or to Phillips, the well-known seafood joint, for one of their famed crab cakes. And no one feels much like going to the aquarium to see the electric eels and leopard sharks and the denizens of the popular tropical rainforest.

Not with the city still teetering on the brink of chaos. Not with so many soldiers and cops lining Pratt Street and staring hard at every car that passes, their index fingers extended ominously close to the triggers on their weapons.

You get the sense of an occupying force, a man named Brad Hutcheson thinks after watching this improbable scene.

Hutcheson, a forty-year-old stay-at-home dad from the nearby neighborhood of Ridgley's Delight, has just returned with his eighteen-month-old son Lex from a stroll to the Inner Harbor. He reports that he was the only parent pushing a child in a stroller, other moms and dads apparently having decided that walking their kids past a gauntlet of edgy, unsmiling troops didn't qualify as family fun.

Hutcheson is unimpressed when he and Lex pause outside the gates for a glimpse of the game. Baseball without fans, he says, "feels like cutting the baby in half. It's like, 'Okay, we're going to have a game. But no one can see it or enjoy it.'"

Nevertheless the rest of the Orioles fans looking on do the things fans always do, even as armored vehicles and military trucks rumble behind them on Camden Street. They chant, "LET'S GO, O'S!" They belt out the signature riff from the White Stripes' "Seven Nation Army"—"OHHH, UH, UH, UH, OHHH, OHHH"—which has become the go-to rallying call for seemingly every fan base in the country.

They clap when the White Sox's batters strike out and jeer them unmercifully as they skulk back to their dugout. They cheer madly when Davis's home run rockets through the clear blue sky and bounces on Eutaw Street, coming to rest forlornly, TV monitors will show, outside a locked men's room door.

In the huge Hilton hotel that rises just behind Camden Yards some one hundred people are watching the game from the fourth-floor courtyard that overlooks the field. A number of other fans have rented rooms and are watching from their balconies, where Orioles banners fly like defiant battle flags.

Paul Dorin, a thirty-seven-year-old sound engineer at a local rock club, has rented room 567 at the Hilton. Along with his friend Chris Pitro he paid $219 for the room, which has a killer view of much of the outfield and an obstructed view of the infield.

There are beer and food up there in the Dorin-Pitro suite. At least a dozen friends are expected to be on hand. The game is blaring from the radio in one part of the room and from the TV in the other part.

"But this is not a celebration," Dorin hastens to explain to the droves of reporters who take the elevator up to his room and pound on his door, looking for color for their stories. Instead, he says, "there's this aspect that you're moving on in spite of the pain in the city."

At times the media contingent covering the fans threatens to outnumber them.

Aside from the team of *Sun* journalists on hand, there are reporters here from the *Washington Post*, the *New York Times*, *USA Today*, and other newspapers, as well as from national cable networks, local TV and radio stations, and various sports websites.

Yet the saturation coverage seems justified in the face of how violent the unrest was and the angry proclamations still being issued by many of the demonstrators and their leaders.

We have no idea when this is going to calm down, thinks Eduardo Encina, the *Sun*'s Orioles beat writer, as he conducts his own interviews with the locked-out fans. *We're prepared for this thing to go on for weeks. You have to be. There's no way to really predict when it's going to end.*

Nevertheless the media circus beyond the gates eventually gets to be too much for Dawn Merguerian, a thirty-five-year-old dentist from Bowie.

Riveted by the spectacle on the field, the normally outgoing Merguerian quickly tires of having microphones, digital recorders, and notebooks thrust in her face while being asked for her thoughts on the game, the riots, the Orioles, the state of the union, and everything else under the sun.

"Listen, can you leave me alone?" she barks to one startled TV reporter. "I'm trying to watch the game!"

Chris Riehl, the thirty-eight-year-old owner of a local tour company, hardly has time to think at all when another reporter rushes up to him and requests an interview.

Before Riehl even has a chance to find out which august media outlet is so interested in his keen observations, the reporter hands him a cell phone and barks: "Here, you're on Sirius Radio!"

Yes, the frenzied 24/7 news cycle is on full display on this sun-dappled slab of sidewalk outside Camden Yards.

And as people like Merguerian and Riehl and the other innocent fans gathered here are discovering, it's not always pretty to see.

17

FROM HIS FRONT-ROW SEAT in the middle of the press box Mark Jacobson gazes out at the peculiar baseball tableau unfolding before him and thinks: *Whoa! It's like I'm having a flashback here . . .*

Jacobson is the game's official scorer today. He's tasked with the all-important business of recording both the significant and ordinary events of the game, as well as making judgment calls on hits and errors, wild pitches and passed balls, and determining which pitcher is credited with the win, the loss, and the save.

But as he takes in all the empty seats his thoughts drift back to a dreary Tuesday night thirty-six years earlier at one of the saddest places on earth back then: Oakland-Alameda County Coliseum any time the Oakland A's took the field.

Hardly anybody went to watch the A's in those years—and with good reason.

They were a singularly awful team, playing in a cold, cavernous concrete eyesore that became known as the "Oakland Mausoleum." They would stumble to a 54-108 record that season, leading pitcher Dave Heaverlo to observe, with only slight exaggeration: "I think we were mathematically eliminated coming out of spring training."

"Everything was terrible," Rich Lieberman, a Bay Area blogger and radio host, said of the A's back then in an interview with Vice Sports. "The amenities were terrible. There were like three things on the menu: there was a hot dog that tasted like it was made with jet fuel in a Moscow whorehouse, and then there was coffee, and then there was Coke."

Not helping matters, their notorious cheapskate owner, Charles O. Finley, had jettisoned payroll, leaving the A's with a roster of rookies, no-names, and never-weres. And, to add insult to injury, Finley was actively shopping the franchise around to any other city that would listen and letting them know that this would be a fire sale.

Oh, yes, Charlie O. made it clear to prospective buyers: no need for deep pockets, folks. Make me an offer. Anything more than a bag of balls, we can talk.

To no one's surprise none of this sat well with the fans. They stayed away in droves. Who would pay good money to watch this train wreck? Especially when it seemed the train wreck itself wouldn't be around for very long?

Well, Mark Jacobson would.

He was a skinny, red-headed graduate student at Stanford at the time. He was also the quintessential baseball nerd. So on the night of April 17, 1979—a chilly, foggy, damp evening with the equally dreadful Seattle Mariners in town for the second game of a four-game series—Jacobson decided he had nothing better to do than to watch the A's.

Yet that feeling, it must be said, did not strike many others in the Bay Area.

The A's would announce that only 653 obviously tormented souls had bought tickets to the game. But less than half that number actually showed up. Those that did, like Jacobson, naturally gravitated to the seats behind home plate. And this cozy seating arrangement, first baseman Dave Revering would say later, made it easier for him to count every single fan—which he actually did.

His tally? Around 250. Plus whoever was hitting the rest rooms and concession stands at the time of this impromptu survey.

It was so quiet in the huge stadium that the outfielders could hear fans ordering Cokes and peanuts.

"I was in the front row talking to two guys who were friends of Bobby Valentine, who was leading off for the Mariners," Jacobson would recall. "You're on a first-name basis with everyone in the ballpark, including the vendors."

In something of a minor miracle the game actually turned out to be exciting. With the bases loaded in the bottom of the ninth, two outs, and the score tied 5–5, catcher Jim Essian shook off the nagging effects of the flu and delivered a walk-off single for a 6–5 A's win.

The attendance figure of 653 would be the lowest in A's history, and the club would go on to average just 3,787 fans per game to rank dead last among Major League teams. Yet thirty-six years later Jacobson looks around at another empty stadium—this one *totally* devoid of fans—that evokes memories of that long-ago evening in the Mausoleum.

That was the least Major-League-like game I've ever seen, he thinks, shaking his head in wonder. *Until now.*

In the rest of the press box close to a hundred reporters from all over the country tap away at their laptops, crack nervous jokes about the unnerving stillness, and attempt to summon adjectives besides "surreal" to describe what they're seeing.

Google's synonym finders are getting so many hits it's a wonder the search engine doesn't crash.

For veteran baseball writer Mel Antonen, here on assignment for sportsillustrated.com, the emptiness of the ballpark takes him back to his childhood in South Dakota.

He grew up in Lake Norden, a tiny town with a population of around 380. His father, Ray, was a livestock feed salesman with a side job that seemed like the coolest in the world to twelve-year-old Mel: delivering vitamins to the Minnesota Twins.

The drive to Metropolitan Stadium in Bloomington in Ray's company car, an Oldsmobile Eighty-eight, took four hours with no traffic. Mel and his dad would leave the house at dawn and get to the stadium by 9:30. Once they were through dispensing vitamins to the star-studded cast in the Twins' clubhouse—this was the 1969 team with Hall of Famers Rod Carew and Harmon Killebrew, as well as Bobby Allison, Cesar Tovar, Mudcat Grant, Dean Chance, and Jim "Kitty" Kaat—the two Antonens would head outside to watch batting practice.

It was then, with the gates still locked hours before the 1:15 p.m. start of weekend games, that they soaked up the sights and sounds young Mel would never forget: the Killer, with his barrel chest and Popeye forearms, launching one pitch after another into the stratosphere, the *CRACK!* of bat meeting ball reverberating throughout the stadium, like a note held by a tuning fork, before it came to slam with a BANG! into the wooden seats in the left-field pavilion. The BING! BING! BING! of a ball landing in the stands and bouncing off the iron railings. The hollow THUNKA! THUNKA! THUNKA! of balls being emptied from a bucket on the mound for the BP pitcher.

There were smells that never left him, too, particularly the lingering scent of pine tar on a warm Minnesota morning, untainted by the odors of nachos, hotdogs, cotton candy, and beer that a packed ballpark exudes. It was all so intoxicating to a baseball-mad kid, watching his heroes in their office, as it were, already toiling away on their workday, in the hours before the gates opened and everyone else could watch them, too.

After seeing the Twins' sluggers drive all those balls into the stands—balls that were just sitting there, practically *begging* to be harvested!—Mel would ask his dad if he could go collect a few.

But the answer was always no.

They had to stay on the field, Ray Antonen said with a shake of his head. That was the rule. And rules were rules.

Yet for Mel Antonen, being at Camden Yards also summons the mixed feelings he had covering another singular event: the '89 World Series, when the Loma Prieta earthquake tore through the San Francisco Bay area and baseball suddenly seemed insignificant.

Just like back then, everyone here is talking about how bizarre this is, he thinks. But no one wants to enjoy it or celebrate it for its historic perspective. As a journalist you kind of put that emotion aside and say: "This is a unique story." But at the same time you want to be respectful and not say: "Hey, this is really bizarre! I'm glad I'm here! This is cool!"

Jonathan Bernhardt is also part of this packed press box. He's a young columnist working as a stringer for *Guardian US*, an offshoot of Britain's well-regarded daily newspaper.

He feels privileged to be here chronicling what he calls "one of the most oddly memorable events in modern baseball history." But, in much the same manner as Antonen, he acknowledges the strange duality of the role the media is playing.

"While a city struggles to hold itself together," he writes, "we watch a baseball game, because it's our job to do so."

Bernhardt also laments the air of frivolity he senses among certain reporters—not from Orioles beat writers and local media, but mainly from the freelancers who have parachuted into Baltimore to cover the riots for national media outlets.

It seems like a social outing to them, he thinks. *Like they're having fun. They're thinking of this as a break, as something to take their minds off what's actually going on in the city with the death of Freddie Gray. And that's not what this is.*

One member of the press corps who shares none of that levity is Rich Dubroff, the seasoned Orioles beat writer for csnmidatlantic.com.

Dubroff lives in Bolton Hill, a residential neighborhood not far from Penn North, with lots of stately three-story row houses with polished marble steps out front.

On the Monday afternoon of the Freddie Gray rioting, he was in the Orioles' clubhouse around three o'clock, watching tv with the players and other reporters as the angry schoolkids poured out of Mondawmin and faced off against the cops.

But Dubroff had a more vested interest in what was going on than anyone else in the room. *Wow,* he thought uneasily as the rocks and bottles flew and clouds of tear gas floated in the streets, *that's not far from my house.*

When the ballgame against the White Sox was cancelled and he tried to make his way home, a ten-minute drive north, the full scope of the violence became clearer. Police in riot gear were everywhere. Store windows were smashed up and down Eutaw Street. Just a couple of blocks away in the strip mall on McMechen Street a grocery store, Rite Aid, laundromat, and hardware store had been looted and vandalized. Reportedly employees there had also been threatened and beaten.

Looking for a parking space in front of his house Dubroff saw a group of young people casually walking down the street carrying what was obviously looted merchandise. He jumped out of the car and hurried inside before the youths noticed him.

He didn't need these kids thinking the middle-aged white guy who just eyeballed them might snitch. There could be heavy retaliation for that sort of thing if they knew where he lived.

(Sure enough, the next time he took his car in for repairs the mechanic pointed out dents caused by someone—possibly those same looters—jumping up and down on the roof.)

All of it shook Dubroff as few things in his life ever had. He and his wife, Susan, a pediatric nurse at a nearby hospital, have lived in the city for twenty-seven years and love it passionately and unequivocally—warts and all.

Susan's mother, Dolores Strachan, had lived with them until her death six months earlier. Dolores was from Michigan. But she too had come to love the city and the interesting, racially diverse neighborhood in which her daughter and son-in-law lived.

As Rich and Susan Dubroff watched the rage on the faces of the protesters captured by the TV cameras and the devastation caused by the rioting, they thought of Dolores and fought back tears.

"Thank God she's not here to see this," they kept murmuring to each other.

Now, as he sits in this overflowing press box covering this freakish baseball game, with the chants of demonstrators audible in the distance, Dubroff can't shake the feeling that the city has been irreparably harmed.

And seeing the National Guard troops this morning, roaring down his street in their sand-colored Humvees as if headed to the front lines of a battle, has him wondering if life in his quiet neighborhood will ever be the same.

He's a pro, able to compartmentalize his growing anxiety as he sits at his laptop and bangs out a game story and side-bars about what he knows to be the strangest day in the history of Baltimore sports. But he senses that he's not the same person he was even thirty-six hours ago, when he watched the sky light up with flames and the worst of the rioting rage so close to his home.

"It just harmed us," he'll say for weeks. "I think about what happened every day. I look over my shoulder more."

Until Monday evening he'd never felt the cold, naked fear he feels about living in the city.

Now he wonders if that fear will ever leave him.

18

JOHN ANGELOS IS IN a pensive mood as the game continues on the lush green field visible from the window in his fifth-floor office in the Warehouse.

Even though he appreciates the oddity and significance of what's taking place below he's putting in a normal work-day, consumed with the seemingly endless responsibilities of a Major League baseball executive. Which means he's only intermittently glancing at the TV in his office for score updates and highlights of the lopsided contest so far.

A soft-spoken, reserved man, the Orioles' executive vice president has suddenly emerged as an unlikely champion of the Freddie Gray protesters—at least the ones who didn't pillage and set stores on fire.

After the violence that erupted near Camden Yards Saturday night Angelos's empathetic tweets about Baltimore's most marginalized citizens have gone viral. He's become a darling of well-known progressives all over the country, such as Ralph Nader and Keith Olbermann. Over two dozen media outlets, including virtually every network and cable news show, have contacted him for interviews.

All this attention is more than slightly bewildering to Angelos.

He has fewer than six thousand Twitter followers, for one thing. And he'd sent out a grand total of 171 tweets before Saturday, in keeping with the low profile he's adopted with the Orioles since his father, Peter G. Angelos, purchased the team in 1993.

And while the response to his twenty-one weekend tweets has been overwhelmingly positive, that, too, has him feeling slightly uncomfortable as the game goes on.

It's a strange thing to be complimented for, he thinks of his tweets, *because you're not the person suffering. You're being commended for something. But you really haven't made any difference in the day-to-day life of people.*

Angelos was in upstate New York on a business trip when protesters first descended on Camden Yards four nights ago and the evening turned violent.

After chaotic skirmishes between protesters and fans broke out at nearby bars, store windows were shattered, and at least five police cars were vandalized by large groups of demonstrators, WBAL-Radio sports-talk host Brett Hollander took to Twitter to talk about how the unrest was disrupting fans attending the Orioles game.

"Everyone should feel fortunate for our freedoms in this country, as written in our Constitution," Hollander began. "I'm by no means a legal scholar, so please understand that, but protests should not violate the basic freedoms of nonprotesters.

"People of a community," he went on, "should be able to commute, commerce should happen, & citizens who want to go to a ballgame should be able to go. And any really important message out of these protests is lost when the rest of the community is disrupted."

None of this sat well with John Angelos.

His wife, Margaret, was driving the two of them on the New York State Thruway north of Albany when he first noticed Hollander's tweets and those of others chiming in. Shortly after 10:30 p.m. he began typing a response on his Blackberry.

So determined was he to use precise language and avoid errors of grammar and punctuation that he asked Margaret to pull over twice so he could concentrate and not worry about tapping an errant key if the car hit a bump.

What followed was an impassioned Twitterstorm that expressed Angelos's frustration that the central message of the protests—and the significance of the uprising—was being lost in any discussion of fan inconvenience at a ballgame.

"Brett," he began, "speaking only for myself, I agree with your point that the principle of peaceful, non-violent protest and the observance of the rule of law is of utmost important in any society. MLK, Gandhi, Mandela and all great opposition leaders throughout history have always preached this precept.

"Further, it is critical that in any democracy, investigation must be completed and due process must be honored before any government or police members are judged responsible.

"That said, my greater source of personal concern, outrage and sympathy beyond this particular case is focused neither upon one night's property damage nor upon the acts, but is focused rather upon the past four-decade period during which an American political elite have shipped middle-class and working-class jobs away from Baltimore and cities and towns around the United States to third-world dictatorships like China and others, plunged tens of millions of good, hard-working Americans into economic devastation, and then followed that action around the nation by diminishing every American's civil rights protections in order to control an unfairly impoverished population living under an ever-declining standard of living and suffering at the butt end of an ever-more militarized and aggressive surveillance state.

"The innocent working families of all backgrounds whose lives and dreams have been cut short by excessive violence, surveillance, and other abuses of the Bill of Rights by government pay the true price, and ultimate price, and one that far exceeds the importance of any kids' game played tonight, or ever, at Camden Yards.

"We need to keep in mind people are suffering and dying around the U.S., and while we are thankful no one was injured at Camden Yards, there is a far bigger picture for poor Americans in Baltimore and everywhere who don't have jobs and are losing economic, civil and legal rights, and this makes inconvenience at a ballgame irrelevant in light of the needless suffering government is inflicting on ordinary Americans."

The 322 words, lacerating in their condemnation of government indifference toward poverty and stirring in their defense of the downtrodden, come as no surprise to those who know Angelos well.

He attended the tony Gilman School, a private prep school in the upscale Baltimore neighborhood of Roland Park, as well as Duke University and the University of Baltimore School of Law.

But the Angelos family has a long history of supporting progressive causes and generously giving to dozens of nonprofits. Peter Angelos, a Democrat, built his reputation—and accumulated his considerable wealth—fighting for the "working man" in thousands of asbestos cases litigated by his well-known law firm.

The elder Angelos, the son of Greek immigrants, grew up working in his father's East Baltimore tavern. He started the Law Offices of Peter G. Angelos in 1961 and, according to friends and associates, soon developed a healthy mistrust—some would say it was more a loathing—of corporate America.

As the majority stakeholder in a group of investors he bought the Orioles in the summer of 1993 and wasted little time showing his pro-labor bona fides. When the players' union went out on strike the following season the Orioles were the only one of the twenty-eight Major League franchises to refuse to hire replacement players.

Little wonder that John Angelos developed a social conscience and a contrarian view of authority at an early age. Both were practically baked into his DNA.

In the hours after his spontaneous tweets about the protesters, though, Angelos worried about two things. He didn't want to be seen as upstaging the turmoil in the streets. And he didn't want his remarks to be taken as an ad hominem attack on the police.

But neither fear materialized. Instead his remarks were lauded by many in the city and around the nation for their nuanced view of the protests and their calmative effect.

Ralph Nader, the long-time political activist, called them "very, very incisive." Before the worst of the rioting on Monday Nader added: "Why does it take a few dozen young people smashing windows in cars to wake up the power structure and start paying attention to the necessities of millions of low-income people all over the country?"

Keith Olbermann, the ESPN2 anchor, was also laudatory, although he mistakenly inflated Angelos's position in the Orioles' hierarchy by noting: "That a sports team owner should make that point, that he should act as if his city and the citizens that city represents, all its citizens, were more than just a name to stick on the team's road uniforms, that is a rare thing indeed."

Many African American leaders, sports figures, and celebrities reacted with delight to Angelos's tweets.

NFL Hall of Famer Thurman Thomas tweeted: "Thank

you sir." Iconic civil rights leader Jesse Jackson, author Wes Moore, and celebrated Baltimore attorney Billy Murphy, representing Freddie Gray's family, applauded the remarks.

So did thirty-year-old Brandon Scott, the youngest member of the Baltimore City Council—and among the most vocal.

Scott, urbane and thoughtful beyond his years, has enormous "street cred" with the youth of Baltimore. And like most black leaders in the city he was hardly shocked when aggrieved demonstrators took to the streets after Freddie Gray's death and tempers boiled over.

"The bigger message to me was that people were no longer going to be ignored, whether they were listened to or not," he's been saying. And the city's power brokers, he added, "were going to willingly listen, or they were going to be forced to listen."

Scott says John Angelos's tweets—like the news-conference love Adam Jones gave to the city's young brothers—signaled to people in Baltimore's poorest neighborhoods that *someone* is listening.

At least they know they're not crying out in a vacuum.

"I thought it was critical for someone in John's position to say what he said because it meant so much," Scott says. "And John's a good guy. He wants to understand."

Just yesterday *Democracy Now!*, the reformist TV, radio, and internet news program, discussed the impact of Angelos's tweets. And today or tomorrow he'll talk with PBS, MSNBC, and CBS *This Morning*, turning down most of the other media outlets clamoring for an interview.

There's another reason Angelos's remarks are attracting so much attention: it's exceedingly rare for a top baseball executive—or a top official of any major sports team—to take a stand on a controversial subject, no matter what it is.

Perpetually terrified of turning off a large portion of their fan base, these execs are loath to weigh in on a subject like a big-city riot that lays bare issues of race and class and heavy-handed police tactics.

Oh, if pressed for a comment by reporters, team officials might issue bland statements designed to offend no one, condemning the violence but saying little else.

Or they might trot out a team spokesperson with a fixed smile to spout vague generalities about the need for the city to heal and come together, hoping no one will notice how little substance their words carry.

Instead John Angelos has given a full-throated defense of the masses who've been peacefully protesting the death of Freddie Gray for days now. But he finds the idea that he's emerged as some kind of folk hero of the left, or the bard of downtrodden Baltimore, more than slightly unreal.

"It's funny," he says, with a soft smile. "No one ever covered *anything* I ever tweeted before."

Yet given his bold and thoughtful comments during this fraught time in his hometown, there's a feeling among many that his Twitter anonymity is about to come to an end.

It's a possibility that does not exactly fill him with joy, even as he hopes this strange baseball game five stories below brings a distraction—and therefore some small comfort—to a ruptured city.

19

UP IN THE MASN booth Gary Thorne and Jim Palmer again show why they're two of the best in the business.

If the typical early-season baseball telecast is a couple of folksy announcers leisurely guiding their viewers through nine innings while joking and making dinner plans off-camera, this one has a completely different feel to it.

Thorne, who has covered everything in his storied forty-eight-year broadcasting career from Major League Baseball to the NHL, the Olympics, and NCAA sports, feels pressure behind the microphone for the first time in ages.

"Or maybe pressure's not the right word," he says. "Maybe it's just more focus."

Whatever it is, he feels the need to put the game in context for viewers, to talk about what drove the Orioles and White Sox to play behind locked gates as though it were being played behind a penitentiary's walls.

He also feels the need to question, during the broadcast, why Baltimore, after all these years, still can't seem to help its most desperate and alienated citizens and so has to deal with this latest spasm of civil disorder.

Palmer, the genetic marvel who appears as youthful as ever at seventy, is of a similar mind as the broadcast unfolds.

"There's something much bigger going on outside the ballpark," he says, and he too feels a desire to vent about the city's seemingly intractable problems.

Above all else the two men are determined to get their call of the game right. They want to make it as informative and entertaining as always. But they also want to help the viewers see and hear and even *feel* how weird this all is: a baseball game that feels encased in shrink-wrap, with so much of the noise and color and emotion bled from it.

When they return from a commercial break in the top of the fourth inning, with the Orioles still up 7–0 and Jimmy Paredes striding to the plate, Thorne hits exactly the right note.

What follows feels almost like a piece of performance art.

"Listen," he instructs the viewers. "Just *listen . . .*"

Then he grows silent.

As does Palmer.

For some seven or eight seconds the MASN audience gets a taste of the ungodly stillness in the ballpark. All that can be heard is the muffled voice of a faraway fan borne on a light breeze blowing in from the gates beyond left field.

"Simon and Garfunkel," Thorne says finally. "The sounds of silence here at Camden Yards for this historic ballgame."

When Palmer likens the atmosphere to a languorous spring

training B game on a back field, he launches into a terrific story of being in just such a contest thirty-three years earlier.

This was in late March 1982 at old Miami Stadium, a blistering concrete saucer topped with a cantilevered roof over the grandstand that had all the charm of a seedy Tijuana racetrack.

It was eleven in the morning when he walked off the mound and spotted a small young woman with spiky black hair and a black leather outfit among the handful of spectators.

"Who's that?" Palmer asked fellow Orioles pitcher Sammy Stewart.

That, Stewart said, is the punk rocker Joan Jett. You don't know her?

No, Palmer didn't. Although the tight black leather look in the sultry tropical heat pretty much guaranteed that it wasn't just an anonymous office worker on her lunch break.

But Joan Jett knew all about Jim Palmer.

As it happened, Jett was a die-hard Orioles fan who had grown up in Rockville, Maryland. When she was introduced to Palmer that morning she told him that her dad had taken her to Baltimore's Memorial Stadium for an Orioles game against the Oakland A's on August 13, 1969. Which just happened to be the day Palmer threw a no-hitter for an 8–0 Orioles win.

"What are you doing here?" Palmer wanted to know.

"Oh, I'm with Sting tonight at the Hollywood Sportatorium," she answered. "Why don't you come up and I'll get you backstage passes?"

The chance to meet the English rocker and his hugely successful punk band, The Police, did not strike the three-time Cy Young Award winner as a bad deal at all.

At the time Palmer was a national spokesman for Jockey underwear with matinee-idol looks and piercing blue eyes. So before parting ways with Jett he traded a poster of himself posing in what he called "the skimpiest briefs on the planet" for a poster of a glowering Jett sitting astride a motorcycle.

And that evening, before Jett and her band, the Runaways, opened for The Police, there was Palmer with young daughters, Jamie and Kelly, chatting up Sting and various other musicians backstage at the venue known as "The Rock Mecca of South Florida."

"Very nice!" Thorne exclaims when the story is over. "So it *does* pay to get up early!"

"Well, it was eleven o'clock . . . ," Palmer answers. Not exactly the crack of dawn.

But the exchange is one of the few light moments the two will have throughout the broadcast.

Both men admit to feeling an overwhelming sadness about what's happened to the city. But they're also a couple of old pros who have been around the game forever. And they still believe in the therapeutic powers of baseball, in the corny notion that something like what they're doing now, bringing a game to life for a viewing audience on a gorgeous spring afternoon, helps people come together—even in a place as roiled as Baltimore.

"I guess this is what we always do in sports during these kinds of moments," Thorne will say later. "We always fall back on: 'Well, baseball's part of the fabric of this country.' And we've gone through this in world wars, we've gone through this after 9/11, we've gone through this during earthquakes.

"At some point we come back and we play. At least we like to tell ourselves that it's meaningful to the regrouping of the city or the nation. I don't know if that's true or not. But that's what we think.

"But that's been the history of the game," he continues. "During the most difficult of times presidents ask that ballgames continue. There seems to be a need for that. And because baseball is cyclical, six months every day, it *does* have a continuum, that whether people recognize it or not, even if they're not fans, this thing, this baseball thing, is going on. And it weaves its way through seven months, if you count spring training, and it's really unlike anything else.

"It's there every day. It's a companion."

In the top of the fifth inning the White Sox finally get to Ubaldo Jimenez—enough to suggest, anyway, that Chicago hasn't totally thrown in the towel.

Adam LaRoche draws a lead-off walk and Avisail Garcia reaches on an infield single to put runners on first and second.

But after Conor Gillaspie flies to left for the first out Thorne and Palmer again feel duty-bound to talk about the tension that hangs over the city.

Thorne gives a shout-out "to the good people of Baltimore who are listening" and sends "our hopes that the city remains calm." He also lauds "all the great people who went out yesterday to clean up Baltimore in the ravaged parts of the city.

"It was a great show of what this city is all about," he concludes. "And hopefully it will remain that way forever."

Chicago gets its first run when Alexei Ramirez hits a bouncer to third that Manny Machado fields and throws past Cabrera at second, the error allowing LaRoche to score. Garcia crosses the plate a moment later on Geovany Soto's ground ball to short to pull the White Sox to within 7–2.

Still, in the quiet White Sox dugout, the thudding realization that there might not be a heroic comeback is beginning to set in.

Jimenez is pitching too well, for one thing. He's showing pinpoint command with his four-seam fastball, getting plenty of movement on his sinker, and mixing his pitches masterfully.

The Orioles are also beginning to loosen up, so much that when Micah Johnson bounces out to Everth Cabrera to end the inning Chris Davis takes the throw at first and playfully lobs the ball into the stands to a group of imaginary fans pleading for it near the Baltimore dugout.

For the Orioles' slugger it proves to be an unexpected emotional release.

He's done the same thing hundreds of times, of course, flipped a ball to some lucky kid with a foghorn voice who's been begging for a souvenir since the game started.

But now, in this hushed ballpark, that simple gesture is almost an act of defiance. He's not trying to show anyone up. But my God! Can't we show a little life?

No one wants to play a baseball game with the seats empty, he thinks when he tosses the ball. *There's no emotion. There's no adrenaline. You don't feel that energy. Maybe that at least will lighten the mood.*

One sure-fire way to lighten it would involve having Buck Showalter reprise the famous bit he did in 1992 on *Late Night with David Letterman*.

This was during Showalter's first year as the manager of the Yankees. Arriving at Yankee Stadium with his producer and a camera crew in tow, Letterman said he was looking for lessons in how to act like a ballplayer.

"We're looking for the subtleties," the talk show host added. "We're looking for the lost art of baseball. I want to look like a player."

Fat chance of that happening.

Nevertheless Showalter, playing the whole thing hilariously deadpan, pretended to teach Dave how to spit so he wouldn't look like a dweeb, and how to utter the mumbled nonsensical phrases of encouragement that pass for chatter.

But there will be none of that here today. From his perch on the right side of the Orioles' dugout Showalter sits with his arms crossed and his game-face on, sensing that a win—the only thing that matters in this strange, sclerotic setting—is well within the Orioles' grasp.

Only when Manny Machado torches poor Samardzija for yet another homer in the bottom of the fifth—his fourth of the young season—to make the score 8–2 does Showalter permit himself the barest perception of a smile

It vanishes in an instant, seconds after Machado slaps his palm and bounds into the dugout. Replacing it is the sense of fatalism that seems to leak into every manager's soul the longer he's around this game.

There is still too much baseball to be played to take anything for granted.

And disaster, as always, lurks around every corner.

20

AT A LITTLE PAST three o'clock there is a stirring amid the exiled, huddled masses watching from behind the closed gates in left field.

A trim, dapper, familiar-looking man has just joined their ranks.

Kweisi Mfume is in the house.

Actually he's locked out of the house, along with everyone else here, so his bonding with the rest of the fans is immediate.

The former Maryland congressman and NAACP president has just come from City Hall, where he did an interview with CNN's Brooke Baldwin on the origins of the simmering tension in the city.

The exchange with Baldwin proved to be fascinating. Many are already calling it one of the most concise, illuminating explanations they've heard for the rage in the streets the past few days.

It began with the CNN anchor recounting that she had walked the streets of West Baltimore earlier that morning with a twenty-four-year-old African American from the neighborhood who talked about why so many young people there run away from the police and distrust them mightily.

"How should the city be reaching out to the youth?" Baldwin asked Mfume. "What would your message be to these young people in the city?"

This one was right in Mfume's wheelhouse and he turned on it quickly, answering in his usual precise and thoughtful manner.

"The city has to have a conversation with communities," he replied. "That's got to occur. People want to express themselves. And we have got to be able to say we understand it. They're not just making this up.

"I grew up here in West Baltimore in that same neighborhood," he continued. "I was arrested thirteen times by the age of nineteen for just standing out on the corner or not moving fast enough when the police came."

Hearing this Baldwin was incredulous.

"Thirteen times?" she said.

"Thirteen times," Mfume answered. "So that's an arrest record. Can you imagine what a conviction record would do to you if you're trying to get a job or something? We feel this. This has been going on for a long, long time. It's been forty-seven years since the city erupted like this. But it's really because of poverty, pain, despair."

"But it hasn't changed," Baldwin observed a moment later.

"People are still paining about the burning of the cvs and the looting that took place," Mfume said, a sad look coming over him. "And they recognize that this is a very small group of people. No, it hasn't changed, but the conditions that created it have not changed, either.

"You cannot expect people to live here . . . in absolute abject poverty in a society that doesn't provide the best social program, which is a job, and in a city where the police department structurally has very serious problems in terms of the way they treat people in the black community.

"And this is not just about black people," he went on. "This is about poor Latinos and poor whites in the city that experience the same sort of harassment oftentimes. And so the good police officers get painted with a broad brush. And the bad ones hide behind the shield."

After ending the interview with a call for an "Urban Marshall Plan" to deal with problems in distressed inner cities all around the country, Mfume walked quickly over to Camden Yards to check on another passion of his: Orioles baseball.

Now here he is, a longtime season-ticket holder, pressing his head against the warm steel bars along Camden Street with dozens of other gawkers, determined to see for himself what this thoroughly bizarre rendition of a big-league game looks and feels like.

He's been listening to it on the radio on the drive to City Hall, and the familiar sounds and rhythms of baseball have allowed him to hope that maybe—just maybe—the worst of the unrest might be over and that the city isn't broken beyond repair.

But this whole scene outside the gates is so overwhelming he can barely process it.

Here's the game that I love, he thinks, shaking his head, *in the city that I love, being played without any fans in the middle of great civil discord and disobedience, and a community crying out for help and attention. There's a lot going on here . . .*

Even as he mingles with the others and grants a quick interview to a reporter from the *Baltimore Sun*, it's plain to see that Mfume is exhausted.

The profound sadness and the intensity of the grief he felt at Freddie Gray's funeral still weigh heavily on him.

Along with other African American community leaders and ministers he's been walking the streets each day for hours since the unrest began, urging the young protesters to keep their hopes and dreams alive and their protests peaceful.

As a longtime civil rights activist he's been a go-to interview for out-of-town journalists like Baldwin and Lester Holt of NBC's *Nightly News*, with whom he walked near a church in East Baltimore destroyed in a suspected arson two nights earlier.

He's also old enough to remember the terrible 1968 riots that engulfed Baltimore after the assassination of Rev. Martin Luther King Jr. Mfume was nineteen back then when Pennsylvania Avenue in West Baltimore descended into chaos.

He remembers the sobbing crowds that flooded into the streets, the furious young men smashing windows and burning stores, the National Guard troops with fixed bayonets outside his home on Robert Street. No wonder his contact info is in the cell phone of every journalist and news show producer in town to chronicle the latest controversial death of a black man in police custody.

But mingling happily now with these banished outcasts from Orioles Nation, his thoughts drift back to the first few times he saw the Orioles play.

This was the ancient year of 1954. The financially strapped St. Louis Browns had just moved to the East Coast to begin play as the Major League Baltimore Orioles at old Memorial Stadium on Thirty-Third Street.

Mfume—born Frizzell Gray—was six years old and living in Turner Station, a black enclave in the southeastern part of Baltimore County. His aunt, a big baseball fan, would pack lunches and the two would travel by bus and streetcar before walking the final blocks up Thirty-Third Street to the game. There they would sit with the other "colored" fans in a remote section of the stands and cheer for Baltimore's newest sports heroes.

At one of those first games his aunt pointed to a dark-skinned pitcher warming up in the bullpen. Voice tinged with pride, she loudly announced: "There's Jehosie Heard!"

Jehosie "Jay" Heard, a diminutive lefty, was the first African American to play for the Orioles in a regular-season game. As was the case when the great Jackie Robinson had broken baseball's color barrier seven years earlier, the quiet Heard was thought to be mentally tough enough to handle the abuse he'd surely receive from racist fans and bigoted ballplayers and managers above and below the Mason-Dixon Line.

To the great disappointment of young Frizzell's aunt Heard didn't get into the game that day. He didn't get into many others either. By June, after pitching in just two games, he was demoted to the Triple-A Portland (OR) Beavers following reports of his role in a domestic disturbance.

Jay Heard never pitched in the Majors again. But the awe-struck kid from Turner Station never forgot the thrill of seeing a man with skin color like his own in an Orioles uniform, and his love for the team would endure for the next sixty-some years.

Standing in the bright sunshine of Camden Street now, Mfume finds himself quietly admiring his hometown team again, this time for everything it's done over the past four volatile days.

He's heartened by the Saturday night tweets of John Angelos that expressed such compassion for Baltimore's most needy citizens. In fact he plans to call his old friend Peter Angelos and tell him: "You raised quite a son there, Pete."

He's also buoyed by the pregame remarks of Adam Jones and Chris Davis and Buck Showalter, who took pains to emphasize that the explosion of violence in Baltimore and the suffering of its citizens were far more important than this game or any other game they would play.

"What I sense," Mfume tells Orioles beat writer Eduardo Encina of the *Sun*, "is that there was an effort here—reading between the lines of many of the players—to give people for two or three hours a sense of normalcy during a very disruptive situation.

"It by no means takes attention away from the real issue. The real issue is justice for the Gray family."

Whenever he *does* manage to get Peter Angelos on the phone Mfume also plans to tell the owner that he and his son did the right thing by having this game played behind locked gates and freeing the police to try and keep the rest of the city calm.

There are other African American community leaders—notably city council president Bernard C. "Jack" Young and council member Nick Mosby, who represents the neighborhoods where the worst of the rioting occurred—who disagree with the Orioles' decision.

They feel the game should have been played as always, with fans in attendance. Show the world that Baltimore's on the rise again, they say. That it's still open for business.

But Mfume doesn't buy that thinking.

How do you square the image of a downtown ballpark filled with cheering fans with a city that was burning less than thirty-six hours earlier?

A city that's still smoldering.

A city with soldiers in the streets and tanks rumbling and angry young men promising that Monday's uprising will look like a fraternity dustup compared to what will happen if the six cops involved in Freddie Gray's arrest aren't indicted.

Even if you hate the trendy phrase about how the optics would look, my God, how would the optics look?

No, Mfume thinks, that wouldn't look good at all. It would make the city appear tone-deaf and clueless, uncaring toward its most vulnerable citizens—even morally bereft.

Still, as he leaves the gawking crowd on Camden Street and walks back to his car, he's feeling more buoyant than he has for days.

It's the middle of the afternoon and the streets are calm so far. In a few green acres of downtown Baltimore, near the blue waters of the harbor, they're playing a baseball game again.

Maybe, he thinks as he climbs behind the wheel, *we'll be all right after all.*

21

TO SEE A FOUL ball sail into the stands at a typical Major League game is to witness a range of fan reactions that can leave one either strangely exhilarated or fearing for the future of mankind.

Sure, there are often great plays to witness: the young dad with a baby snoozing in his lap who casually reaches up and snags a scorching line drive before it can decapitate the seven-year-old sitting next to him. The woman who watches a ball clank pathetically off her husband's stone hands and somehow snares it with her tub of popcorn. The beer vendor who catches a pop-up with his cap while simultaneously passing two Bud Lights down a row of thirsty customers.

But there can be a seamy side to this ritual too.

Witness the grown men with $300 gloves who elbow aside little kids to get at foul balls. Or the lunatics who fall out of the upper decks and hurt themselves—or worse—lunging over railings to snag a keepsake. Or the frat bro whose highlight-reel catch results in his nachos splattering all over the nice grandma in front of him.

The same sketchy dramas can play out after home runs, of course.

Who hasn't seen—either in person or via ESPN highlights—the nightly footraces between beered-up fans in the empty reaches of a stadium, clambering over seats and suffering comic pratfalls in order to reach a ball, launched by Chris Davis or Mike Trout or Bryce Harper or some other hairy-knuckled slugger, that landed three sections away?

Yes, if you're ever keen to see the humiliating lengths people go to in order to snag a souvenir baseball, just go to You-Tube. You'll be shaking your head in no time.

But on this day at Camden Yards there is none of the fan frenzy that normally accompanies this timeless ritual.

The fact is that the only ones going after balls in the stands are a pair of middle-aged men named Rick Rutherford and Perry Sauers. And both move around the venerable ballpark at a distinctly unhurried pace.

Rutherford and Sauers are working for the Orioles as part of the Major League Baseball Authentication Program. They're charged with verifying the authenticity of game-used items such as bats, balls, and jerseys that will later be auctioned off for charity or kept by the Orioles to be displayed for historical value.

And, clearly, there is no doubt that history is being made today.

Which is why Rutherford, a fifty-four-year-old former Baltimore police captain and SWAT team member—authenticators are either retired or active off-duty law enforcement officers—is ensconced in a camera well near the Orioles' dugout, busily going about his job.

He might have the best seat in the house. But Rutherford has been doing this since the program ramped into its present form in 2006; he long ago lost any sense of awe in his surroundings.

As a longtime baseball fan he's aware of the singular nature of the drama taking place here and his small role in it. But as an ex-cop for twenty-six years and a Baltimorean, he's profoundly saddened by the spate of violence that has gripped the city.

Nevertheless he thinks the Orioles and MLB made the right decision to play, even if only for the symbolism it conveys.

Maybe it's not quite business as usual in Baltimore, he thinks, gazing around the vacant ballpark. *But they're letting people know the whole town isn't on lockdown.*

The thought fills him with a sense of optimism that he lacked even an hour ago when he first arrived at Camden Yards. It also enables him to turn his full attention to the task at hand, which is formidable.

Over nine innings he and Sauers will authenticate around a hundred items, everything from a shattered bat to lineup cards to game tickets bought by players for family members, which the players now want as keepsakes.

The two will authenticate seventeen balls put in play throughout the course of the game, including the home run balls hit by Chris Davis and Manny Machado, as well as thirteen foul balls. They'll do the same with three sets of bases, which will be changed every three innings in recognition of the landmark circumstances of the game.

To each item Rutherford and Sauers affix a special hologram, complete with a bar code and a set of numbers that are plugged into a database. Other info—for instance the pitcher and batter involved with a homer or foul ball—is also noted. Whoever takes possession of the keepsake down the road can then go to a website to learn the item's history.

Perhaps most comforting of all: any attempt by, say, a sleazy memorabilia dealer to peel off the hologram will backfire; the hologram will automatically disintegrate.

All of this heightened attention to the legitimacy of game-used items—even ones from a contest with no fans—stems from a massive FBI investigation in the late 1990s nicknamed Operation Bullpen.

It revealed that as many as 75 percent of all baseball autographs were fake, as was a huge percentage of all the sports memorabilia on the market. And it opened up dozens of part-time jobs for men and women like Rutherford and Sauers—a Howard County, Maryland, police officer—who enjoy being close to the game, even in such an unusual capacity.

At least two authenticators, hired as independent contractors, work each of the 2,430 regular-season Major League games, as well as spring training, the All-Star Game, and postseason games.

Now, with Rutherford largely confined to the dugout camera well, it has fallen to Sauers to roam about the vast, desolate ballpark, looking under tarps and seats and in concourse walkways for any balls that land there.

According to director Michael Posner, the Authentication Program likes using law enforcement personnel because of their attention to detail and their knowledge of how to preserve evidence from a crime scene. And as Rutherford and Sauers know from experience, no item at today's game is too big or too small to be authenticated.

When the Orioles clinched the division title a year earlier Sauers and a colleague watched the ritual champagne-spraying in the home team's clubhouse from a spot along one wall. After the celebration they quietly collected the dozens of champagne bottles as well as the corks that came with each. (The bottles went for between $50 and $100 in online auctions. The corks sold for around $25.)

A year before that Rutherford had watched Boston Red Sox slugger David Ortiz go thermonuclear and obliterate a Camden Yards dugout phone with a bat after striking out. The shattered phone wound up with an MLB hologram. So did some of the metal and plastic slivers that Big Papi sent flying in all directions during his temper tantrum.

Happily there are no such violent histrionics in the hushed stadium today. Players in this awkward setting are on their best behavior toward everyone: umpires, opponents, and even the two civilians painstakingly doing their jobs so that collectors of today's memorabilia trove might one day sleep easily, knowing the stuff is legit.

Rutherford works briskly as the balls, bats, and other items to be authenticated pile up, the chatter in the dugout serving as a strange sort of background music to his labors.

He's used to being this close to the action, of course. But normally, when the stadium is packed with fans and the music from the sound system blares, he's only able to hear snatches of conversations in the Orioles' dugout.

Today he can hear *everything*.

He hears every quiet exchange between the players, every cough, every sniffle, every splash of spittle and chew on the concrete floor. He hears every grunt made by Chris Davis as he swings the bat, the rustle of Chicago catcher Geovany Soto's shin guards as he squats, the playful back-and-forth between Caleb Joseph and plate ump Jerry Layne that sounds so clear it's as if he's eavesdropping on a conversation between two men at a bar.

The noise made by the players' spikes as they churn up the first base line after a routine groundout sounds like a thresher at work. In all the years he's been around it Rutherford has never felt so close to the game.

All the sights and sounds of baseball—the unalloyed sights and sounds—seem magnified and wondrous without the crowd noise in the background and the shouts of the vendors snaking through the stands.

The look on Rutherford's face says it all: he's thrilled to be here. And overcome with gratitude. How many people have ever experienced a big-league game like this? And one that counts in the standings, no less!

How many, especially, get to see moments like this up close? When Adam Jones pops out of the dugout lugging his bat, the dozens of fans behind the locked left-field gates explode in cheers.

This is followed by excited cries of, "Jonesy, we love you!" and, "Jones, hit it here, dude!"

Jones hears them and shakes his head.

That last request, he knows, poses a massive logistical problem for two reasons.

Number one, the fans are so far away they might as well be in a different zip code. Paul Bunyan couldn't hit it there. Roy Hobbs and his legendary bat "Wonderboy" couldn't hit it there, never mind a mere mortal like Adam LaMarque Jones.

Man, I couldn't hit it there if I was standing in center field, he thinks.

If anything, though, reason number two is even more insurmountable.

"How am I gonna hit it there," he mutters, looking at Rutherford, "when I'm the one who's *on deck*?"

Hearing this Rick Rutherford can't help cracking up.

Now Jones is smiling, too, even as he chomps on his gum and blows one of his trademark huge bubbles.

It's a deliciously absurd moment in a game that has raised absurdity to new heights, and both men seem grateful for it.

22

OUTSIDE THE BALLPARK A numbness seems to have settled over the city. It feels as if all of Baltimore is attempting to come to grips with the enormity of the violence and destruction it has seen.

If a populace can be said to collectively work through the so-called five stages of grief, then Baltimoreans are well through the denial, anger, and bargaining phases, and dealing somewhat unsteadily with their depression and acceptance of what has happened.

Schools are back in session after Tuesday's closures. But National Guard troops and police in riot gear ring Mondawmin Mall, ground zero for Monday's notorious "Purge." Military Humvees with camouflage markings are posted nearby at Frederick Douglass High School, to the exasperation of many who drive by.

Inside Douglass, students, teachers, and administrators alike are frustrated and angry over the negative publicity the school has endured the past two days from seemingly every media outlet in the area.

Douglass has a proud and enduring legacy. It's the second-oldest U.S. high school created specifically for African American students. It boasts former Supreme Court Justice Thurgood Marshall as one of its most distinguished alumni.

But the school has struggled for years as the poverty, joblessness, and crime in West Baltimore have worsened. Now it's listed among the twenty lowest-performing schools in the state. And since so many of the young people in Monday's initial rock-and-bottle-throwing confrontations with the police were seen wearing the Douglass uniform of light orange shirt and khaki pants, the school is being singled out as the nexus of the unrest.

Even though its defenders point out that some seven hundred of the school's nine hundred students stayed in class rather than join the walkout—and even though kids from other city schools joined in the "Purge"—it's the Douglass kids who are being painted as the thuggish instigators.

Now, on this first day back, reporters from all over have swooped down on the school. City schools CEO Gregory Thornton and teachers with T-shirts reading "One Douglass" are there to welcome students with broad smiles and reassuring hugs.

Celebrities like former Baltimore Ravens great Ray Lewis and the rapper Wale are here, too, telling students to keep their heads up, that better days are ahead, that the entire city is thinking about them and praying for them.

But the Douglass kids are not so easily assuaged.

They're media savvy. Perception is reality—they know this. The school's reputation has taken a major hit. This is underscored shortly after the doors open, when interim principal Iona Spikes takes to the PA system, her voice leaden with emotion as she addresses her charges.

"I believe in all of you . . . it is the reason I am here," she says, as reported by the *Baltimore Sun*. "My heart is heavy! And to be honest, I am angry! The few students who made poor choices cast a dark cloud over Douglass."

There is a new development in the Freddie Gray case that is also keeping tensions simmering.

At a news conference, Baltimore police announce that their initial report on Gray's death will not be released publicly, citing the need to protect the integrity of the inquiry. Instead it will be turned over to Baltimore City State's Attorney Marilyn Mosby, a thirty-five-year-old African American who has been on the job a mere four months.

Mosby is now tasked with the monumental challenge of determining whether any of the officers involved in Gray's arrest will face criminal charges, ensuring that the national spotlight will be trained on her and her colleagues for many weeks to come.

At the same time dozens of protesters arrested in the unrest of the last four days are being released without charges as police admit they are unable to complete the necessary processing paperwork on time.

A notable exception, though, is the case of eighteen-year-old Allen Bullock. The photograph of an enraged Bullock wielding an orange traffic cone and smashing the windshield of a police car four nights earlier near Camden Yards has become a lasting symbol of the Freddie Gray turmoil.

Bullock's photo wound up on the front page of the Sunday *Sun* and was soon picked up by news organizations all over the country. Due in large part to his newfound notoriety he's been slapped with bail of $500,000 and sits forlornly in a Baltimore jail cell with few prospects for getting out anytime soon.

Gov. Larry Hogan and Baltimore mayor Stephanie Rawlings-Blake make a number of public appearances in West Baltimore, where the streets are mostly quiet.

On his way to a meeting with NAACP officials, who detail the economic concerns of the community and its fraught relations with police, Hogan even stops to shoot baskets with a few young men.

He goes 0 for 5 from the foul line and clanks an eighteen-footer from the corner on one of his last shots. But he shows good form on his jumper and his relaxed demeanor and self-deprecating humor—"I better leave before I embarrass myself"—wins over onlookers.

A man in a camouflage cap and shirt shakes his hand and thanks him for coming.

"Very few governors come to meet us," the man says softly, an understatement that provokes grins among the trailing reporters.

Rawlings-Blake is having a far tougher time connecting with her constituents.

Some are still put off by her labeling of the demonstrators as "thugs." Others have accused her of seeming distant and withdrawn in the immediate aftermath of the unrest, an assertion that seems to pain her above all others.

"I'm passionate about my city," she tells reporters. "It concerns me that the people I care about don't know what's in my heart."

After school lets out hundreds of high school and college students from across the city march, mostly peacefully, from Penn Station to City Hall, where a large rally is scheduled to take place. Their cries of, "Justice for Freddie Gray!" and, "Black lives matter!" carry on the light breeze to nearby Camden Yards, adding yet another odd sensory element to the ballgame taking place inside.

The students say they're determined to distance themselves from the demonstrators who rioted Monday and to show the media—and by extension the rest of the country and the whole world—that the young people of Baltimore care about their city.

Yet the lingering questions about Gray's death and the issue of how police treat African Americans in the city's poorest neighborhoods are at the forefront of the protest. Ending the state law known as the Law Enforcement Officers Bill of Rights, which affords legal protection to cops involved in misconduct investigations, is a favorite cause of many in the crowd.

When city council member Brandon Scott leaves his fifth-floor office to talk to the demonstrators, he finds the crowd's mood to be "all over the place."

"Folks were upset. Folks were frustrated," he says later. "But folks were also hopeful. People are mad that a young man died, and that folks have not been listening to them for decades.

"But people were excited, too. Because they felt that people who didn't care about the city now care about the city. And people who didn't understand what it meant to be a poor kid in West Baltimore now want to try to understand as much as possible. So there was a sense of hope as well."

As the crowd at City Hall continues to grow, marches in solidarity with the Freddie Gray protesters are taking place all over the country—organized in no small part by the ever-churning power of social media.

In New York crowds, still angry over the chokehold death of Eric Garner on Staten Island nine months earlier, mass in Union Square and Times Square and disrupt traffic at the Holland Tunnel and the West Side Highway.

In Washington DC, young protesters. take over an H Street intersection near Chinatown before heading on to the White House. There President Barack Obama, who has resisted calls to intervene in the Freddie Gray unrest, calls for a national "soul-searching" on the "slow-rolling crisis" of police encounters with young black men.

Boston, Cincinnati, Minneapolis, Oakland, Philadelphia, Seattle—all are scenes of similar protests and disruptions.

In other parts of Baltimore small attempts are being made to calm jittery citizens and get on with life.

The Charm City Comedy Festival—who needs laughs more than a city reeling from a calamitous riot?—vows to continue its five-day run with a reduced number of acts and earlier start times, so that showgoers can comply with the citywide curfew.

Various theater groups and movie houses juggle their show-times in response to the curfew. And the Baltimore Museum of Industry, housed in an 1860s oyster cannery along the downtown waterfront, offers free admission in an attempt to lure skittish customers back.

Not all activities go on as scheduled. The venerable Flow-erMart, Baltimore's traditional rite of spring famous for lemon-peppermint sticks, ladies in ornate hats, arts and crafts, and more flowers than a thousand mob funerals, is postponed for the first time since its inception in 1911.

But outside the Meyerhoff Symphony Hall, a scant three miles from Mondawmin Mall, perhaps the most singular act of hope and redemption takes place: a free noontime performance by the Baltimore Symphony Orchestra. Billed as a concert for peace, it attracts an appreciative crowd of one thousand.

Fifty-two years earlier, following the assassination of President John F. Kennedy, Leonard Bernstein, the New York Philharmonic music director, had vowed: "This will be our reply to violence: to make music more intensely, more beautifully, more devotedly than ever before."

In that same spirit BSO musicians have donated their time to help the city heal. A day earlier their renowned music director, Marin Alsop, had taken to Facebook to write: "I am heartbroken for our dear city."

Yet today, when she takes the microphone in the bright sunshine and gazes out at the diverse crowd and all the faces smiling back at her, her spirits seem buoyed.

"Music has this incredible power to bring us together," she says.

"Thank you, BSO! Thank you, BSO!" the crowd chants.

When the orchestra launches into the first familiar notes of "The Star-Spangled Banner," the stirring anthem penned by Francis Scott Key in Baltimore Harbor over two hundred years ago, Alsop's words seem prescient.

At first the crowd seems unsure how to react. But within seconds people are leaping to their feet and singing along, many with hands over their hearts.

In the customary homage to the Orioles they yell, "O!" at the words "Oh, say does that star-spangled banner yet wave?"

By the end their singing has become a full-throated roar of defiance—as well as a cry for affirmation.

Their city is down but not out. It will not be defined by a single spasm of strife, no matter how ruinous and disheartening.

And neither, their singing says, will they.

23

AT CAMDEN YARDS, WHERE the Orioles still hold a comfortable 8–2 lead over the White Sox, the game's latter innings feel otherworldly.

In the top of the seventh Ubaldo Jimenez takes no time at all to mow down the White Sox in order.

Adam LaRoche strikes out swinging on an eighty-four-mile-per-hour fastball that drops wildly at the last second. Avisail Garcia strikes out looking on a fastball that catches the outside corner of the plate. Connor Gillaspie swings at the first pitch he sees and lifts a harmless fly ball to left for the third out.

All of this efficiency is making the Orioles' righty—still smarting from the boos he's regularly received from fans—look like a Cy Young Award winner. It does not hurt Jimenez's cause, of course, that the White Sox are up there hacking as if they have dinner reservations to get to.

There seems to be an even more pronounced desire to get this over with on their part. Showing discipline at the plate, looking for your pitch, working the count—all of that is for another day when baseball is baseball again instead of, well, whatever this ungodly thing is that they're playing.

Right now their hurried, feeble swings suggest: It's time to blow this popstand.

As Jimenez walks off the mound and heads slowly to the dugout knowing his work day is over, he's overcome with conflicting emotions.

This, he knows, was his best outing in a long time. He did more than live up to the hoary cliché of giving his team a chance to win. But with so many people hurting and sadness practically seeping out of much of the city, he's not about to whoop and pump his fists and have that be the screenshot they see in Penn North and East Baltimore.

If anyone in those two places is even paying attention to this game.

His teammates welcome him with smiles and fist bumps and high-fives. But even as he towels off and plops down on the bench his thoughts turn to what's happening out on the streets.

Besides baseball we have a life, he thinks. *And this is our city. We get to feel everything everyone else is feeling right now. Who's feeling good right now? Not too many, I'm guessing . . .*

Right before a commercial break Gary Thorne advises the MASN audience: "Now the most unusual seventh-inning stretch in the history of baseball. There is nobody to get up and stretch."

Mercifully Orioles officials have ignored Gordon Beckham's joking suggestion that a player should be nominated to sing "God Bless America."

Instead "Take Me Out to the Ballgame" blares as usual over the sound system. But today it feels almost like a cruel joke, as if all the joy and longing were leached out of baseball's unofficial anthem.

No, there will be no crowds to share the day with, no peanuts and Cracker Jack to be savored. No root-root-rooting for the home team either.

As always "Thank God I'm a Country Boy" quickly follows and somewhere John Denver is rolling over in his grave.

The legendary pop singer's ode to the redneck life is a proud seventh-inning staple at Orioles games. Normally it has fans hooting and yee-hawing and stomping their feet as if at the world's biggest hoedown.

But today as the lyrics reverberate throughout the ballpark, rife with images of a laid-back life on the farm, there's not even a bored sportswriter tapping along with a pen.

All of it, the stillness, the lack of energy, the one-sided game, finally becomes too much for Thorne. After Chicago reliever Scott Carroll gets Delmon Young on a ground ball to short for the first out in the bottom of the seventh, the veteran broadcaster decides to have a little fun.

"Now we talked today, because nobody's in the yard, about the appropriate way to broadcast," he tells his audience. "So with Adam Jones coming up here in the seventh inning . . ."

Here his voice takes on the hushed reverential tones of a golf announcer:

"Jones's approach to the plate with Carroll delivering . . . Jones will whack the son of a gun to center field. That's very deep . . . It's deep and it's off the base of the wall.

"He will head to second base . . . Adam Jones has a double. And that green jacket is well within reach, Jim."

If there is still anyone in the viewing audience who needs further edification of the grand lunacy of what has just transpired, Thorne adds helpfully: "That was my Masters voice."

"I knew you were gonna do it," Palmer says as his booth partner cracks up.

"Look," Thorne explains, "Dawn, our producer, she emails me this morning and says, 'Okay, what voice are you gonna use? Will it be the Masters voice? Or will it be your FREE BASEBALL FOR EVERYBODY! voice?'

"I had no idea," he continues. "I hadn't even had coffee yet! How did I know?"

There is a second or two of silence as Palmer absorbs this new information.

"Well, I'm certainly not going to do my Gary McCord and tell them how slick the greens are," Palmer says finally, referring to McCord's infamous banishment from CBS's Masters TV coverage years earlier for saying the greens were as slick as "bikini wax."

Thorne's golf bit has clearly lifted the spirits of both men and energized the broadcast at just the right time.

So does something else that comes right on its heels.

When Chris Davis flies to left for the second out of the inning Thorne reads a text he's received from Suzyn Waldman, the longtime color commentator on New York Yankees radio broadcasts.

"Six runs in the first inning?" it reads. "Buck will never allow a fan back in the building!"

When Showalter calls the bullpen to get reliever Kevin Gausman up and warming, the ringing of the phone over four hundred feet away sounds like a fire alarm. And when Machado hits a sharp grounder to second to end the inning, Thorne and Palmer are still chuckling over Waldman's tongue-in-cheek jab at the superstitious Orioles manager.

Waldman, however, happens to be dead wrong about Showalter's thinking.

Six-run inning or no—and the Orioles actually just had one in their Sunday shellacking of the Red Sox—this is not the kind of game Showalter wants to see on a regular basis. Or ever again, for that matter.

And the reason is simple: it completely robs the Orioles of home-field advantage.

Showalter is probably the most meticulously prepared manager in baseball. And he's been that way since his first big-league gig with the New York Yankees in 1992, when he was the youngest manager in the Majors.

He's constantly looking for any new strategy, any scrap of information, any intel on the strengths and weaknesses of opposing players that can give the Orioles an edge over other teams.

This near-neurotic attention to detail has paid big dividends: the Orioles are coming off their best season in seventeen years and their first American League East title since 1997. And their scrappy little field leader was just named Manager of the Year for the third time in his brilliant career.

When it was first announced that today's game would be held behind locked gates without fans, Showalter was initially stunned. But, as always, his competitive juices quickly kicked in.

Okay, he thought, *how does that affect our ability to win or lose the game? What do we need to get ahead of? What's going to be different? What's batting practice going to be like? Is there going to be walk-up music? Are the commercials between innings going to be longer?*

Still, he knows all the advance prep in the world can't change this simple fact: without twenty or thirty or forty thousand people in the stands cheering for the Orioles and providing emotional energy, you can pretty much say it's the visiting White Sox who have the advantage in this game.

The way Showalter sees it, they're practically catching the Orioles in a neutral ballpark.

In the top of the eighth, after Gausman strikes out Alexi Ramirez on a ninety-six-miles-per-hour fastball at the knees and Geovany Soto steps into the batter's box, Thorne returns to the topic of playing games without fans in attendance.

He recalls a long-ago article in *Sports Illustrated*—maybe from the 1960s?—when Boston Celtics great Bill Russell was quoted as saying: "Someday, the NBA will play all of its games in a studio. It will be built for basketball. Because that's where the money comes from. It's TV revenue. Won't need fans."

"I think Bill was wrong about that," Thorne declares. "Fans have a tremendous impact on *all* sporting events. But I thought of that today and what it would be like if every game was played in an empty studio built for baseball."

After Soto strikes out Palmer chimes in on the prospect of fanless games, largely echoing Buck Showalter's thoughts.

"Well, you lose a lot of the intrinsic values as a franchise," he says. "Your home-field advantage . . . if you talk to people who had to play against the Russells and Cousys and the Havliceks, Tom Heinsohn, they'll all tell you, 'Well, there were dead spots on the floor in Boston, it was like playing in ninety-eight-degree temperatures.'

"But *that's* your home-field advantage," he continues, speaking of the Celtics. "They knew where the dead spots were."

"And they knew where the heat and the thermostat were," Thorne adds.

"Exactly," says Palmer. "But fans . . . I still remember last year when [the Orioles] clinched [the AL East title]. Thirty-nine thousand people in orange. You don't ever forget those things."

Gausman gets Adam Eaton on a ground ball to second and the White Sox go down in order. They're only three outs away now from ending this ignominious drubbing and fleeing this troubled, God-forsaken town.

Up in the press box, in a nod to Major League Baseball's obsessive fondness for protocol and its need to dot all the i's and cross all the t's with its record-keeping, the PA system crackles to life.

The voice of Orioles media relations manager Jim Misudek fills the room.

"Today's paid attendance is . . . ," he begins, and now there is a dramatic pause worthy of an Oscars presentation, "zero."

One of the ushers duly notes this on the whiteboard that also lists the lineups for both teams and other vital info, such as gametime temperature, time of first pitch, time of game, and the names of the umpiring crew.

The big orange "0" on the board looks so unreal that media members and press-box ushers alike snap photos of it on their cellphones, recording the history-making figure for posterity.

They do this because they know the nature of these sorts of spectacles.

Even though there are only some 110 people shoehorned into the press box, it's a sure bet that years from now hundreds more will claim that they, too, worked the strangest baseball game ever played.

In fact, human nature being what it is, no one would be surprised if hundreds of Orioles fans will come out of the woodwork one day and insist that they, too, stood behind the locked green gates in a riot-torn town to support their team.

If, as has been suggested, the business of sports is to get us to share unique emotional experiences, this game surely qualifies for all who are here right now.

24

WITH ZACH BRITTON ON the mound for the Orioles in the ninth inning, the end comes swiftly—if not mercifully—for the White Sox.

The lefty closer, coming off a productive 2014 season in which he notched thirty-seven saves, is a study in concentration, with his game face firmly in place. It's one of the great game faces of our time, too, a unique study in contrasts. With his youthful, chubby cheeks, light stubble, and scowl, he looks more like a sixteen-year-old who's just had the car keys taken away than one of the most menacing relievers in the game, with an absolutely filthy sinker.

Britton is in now strictly to get some work; it's obviously not a save situation. He's been marveling at the ballpark's muted atmosphere since the game began. Out in the bullpen he could hear every word being said in the Orioles' dugout, almost every snippet of conversation in the press box.

But as he faces his first batter he finds the quiet more unnerving than fascinating. This is especially so when he goes into his windup and picks up Gary Thorne's play-by-play from up in the MASN booth: "So Britton trying to wrap it up here . . . his first pitch will be taken up high . . ."

Luckily Britton doesn't have to be too fine today—the White Sox batters still seem eager to help him out.

Emilio Bonafacio, batting for Eaton, leads off with a sharp single to right. But Melky Cabrera quickly grounds out to second base, and Jose Abreu swings at the first pitch and hits a bouncer to short for the second out.

With Ubaldo Jimenez smiling broadly on the top of the dugout steps and the remaining fans behind the left-field gates loudly chanting, "LET's GO, O's! LET's GO, O's!" Britton goes to work on Adam LaRoche.

He does not have to work for long. He strikes him out on four pitches, the last a sweeping curve that seems to break somewhere around first base. The lefty-batting Chicago DH flails at it and misses by a foot.

And just like that it's over.

Final score: Baltimore 8, Chicago 2.

Time of the game: a snappy two hours and three minutes, far different from the usual MLB games, which too often are interminable slogs lasting three and a half hours or more.

Given the grim humor that spews regularly from the press box you half expect one of the hard-bitten sportswriters to crack: "If it shaves an hour and a half off games, maybe we need more riots."

But the harrowing images of a city unraveling are still fresh in everyone's minds and no sick one-liners are heard. The only sounds are the quiet tapping of laptop keys as reporters file their early game stories before heading downstairs for postgame interviews.

As Caleb Joseph bounces from behind the plate to congratulate Britton and the rest of the Orioles slap hands near the pitcher's mound, "Orioles Magic (Feel It Happen)" blares over the sound system.

The rousing tune has been a team anthem for years. It was inspired by the great 1979 Orioles team, which thrilled fans with a mystical season of come-from-behind wins that culminated in a trip to the World Series. (The Orioles would go on to lose in seven games to the Pittsburgh Pirates, who that year drew on their own inspirational song, Sister Sledge's disco hit "We Are Family.")

But in an empty ballpark in a town scarred by civil unrest, the catchy melody and celebratory lyrics of "Orioles Magic" feel oddly out of place.

Not that the White Sox are listening anyway. Seconds after LaRoche goes down swinging they gather up their equipment in the dugout and quickly retreat to their clubhouse.

When the doors are opened to reporters the Chicago players look weary and distracted. Despite being in full "getaway day" mode—hurrying through interviews and showers to catch their flight to Minnesota for a four-game series against the Twins—they acknowledge to a man that they just had their butts kicked and that their heads were elsewhere.

"The city was on everyone's minds," Adam Eaton tells reporters. "You've just got a lot of emotions running through your mind. As baseball players, as teams, you feed off energy. And when there's nothing there, it's a very surreal and weird moment that I'll never forget—but I kind of wish I could."

White Sox manager Robin Ventura, normally affable and easygoing, is clearly drained.

The look on his face says he enjoyed this about as much as he enjoyed the infamous '93 beat-down he took from Texas pitcher Nolan Ryan, when the then-Sox infielder was drilled on the elbow, charged the mound, and quickly found himself in a killer headlock, with the future Hall of Famer pummeling him unmercifully.

"Today started off bad and got worse," Ventura says. "It was just a weird day. I don't think we really want to play another one like this. I don't think they do either."

The Orioles, as might be expected, are in a far more exuberant mood.

It's been an emotional five days for all of them. And the fact they were able to grind it out and demolish the White Sox under such trying circumstances is uplifting.

There's a sense, too, that this whole awful trial by fire has helped bring this already close-knit team even closer together. At least that's the theory being advanced by Chris Davis, whose three-run blast helped the Orioles put the game away early.

"I think maybe subconsciously," Davis will say later, "there was this thought: okay, there's lot of stuff going on around here, we had to do something we're not necessarily thrilled about doing, playing under these circumstances, but you know what? We play in Baltimore.

"We're not freaking everyday run-of-the-mill Joes. We're tough. It was a point of pride. We're not going to sit here and watch what's going on and hear what's being said and just take it in stride. We're going to do something about it.

"I'm so proud and happy for our guys, for the fans, for the people of Baltimore. I hope something good, something positive came out of this. I hope people were able to experience some normalcy, for even just a few hours."

Looming over Davis and his teammates, of course, is a trip to Tampa and the three upcoming "home" games at Tropicana Field. The domed "Trop," perennially listed as the very worst stadium in the Major Leagues, has all the charm of a sprawling airplane hangar.

Then again it also offers horrible traffic, poor sightlines, lousy food, weird catwalks that ring the rafters and interfere with balls in play, and sparse crowds that appear to be there to catch up on their cellphone video games.

But the Orioles are in too good a mood right now to think about all that. Davis, though, senses that they're all going to be toasted when the adrenaline and the warm glow of winning wear off.

Because once you finally get through something like this and savor it, he thinks, *it's almost like a crash.*

He and Tommy Hunter are already planning to wind down with a few beers this evening on the balcony of one of their condos. And with the tenuous calm in the city somehow holding, neither man will likely feel the need to be cradling a weapon this time.

For the first time in days Davis can feel the tightness in his chest begin to loosen.

25

EVEN AS THE ORIOLES congratulate themselves on grinding out a win and the thoughts of the White Sox turn to whatever is being served for the inflight meal, a compelling new drama is unfolding in the bowels of Camden Yards.

It stars a smart, ambitious Baltimorean named Kendall Hilton, a twenty-five-year-old African American who has made his way to Buck Showalter's postgame press conference with the vague notion of being a provocateur.

Hilton operates a website called Fan-I Sports. He loves America's games and the energy that crackles when passionate fans get together to watch, dissect, and argue about the athletes they love—or loathe.

Feeling that ESPN and similar websites have become too bland and watered down, he's vowed to make Fan-I Sports punchier and more relevant to today's youth. A high school graduate who didn't go on to college, he's been taking writing classes and studying how veteran sportswriters develop and structure their stories. He's also been poring over the *Associated Press Stylebook*, the bible of English grammar and usage for American journalists.

Yet the truth is, he's not even supposed to be here today.

Hilton was originally issued a press credential to cover the Monday game between the Orioles and White Sox. That was his first time ever in the Camden Yards press box. Rubbing elbows with sportswriters and broadcasters he had admired from afar for years, he was beyond excited.

That afternoon, before the game was officially postponed, he watched on the press box TVs with many other reporters as the disturbances around Mondawmin Mall intensified and the standoff between the mostly school-age kids and cops grew uglier.

Then came a not-so-subtle reminder, as if Hilton needed it, of the fractured racial fault lines that have always existed in Baltimore. As the cameras zoomed in on the crowds of angry rock-throwing demonstrators, a white woman standing next to Hilton remarked: "Maybe they should hose them down."

A couple of white police officers nearby chuckled knowingly.

Hearing this, Hilton was incredulous. All three were literally within an arm's length of him, a young African American just like the ones venting their long-simmering frustrations in the streets.

What was going on here? Was he *invisible*?

Was that why the woman and the cops would utter such an insensitive remark in his presence?

And was the woman serious?

Was she really advocating a return to the early days of the Civil Rights Movement, when police in places like Alabama and Mississippi used high-pressure fire hoses—and snarling attack dogs as a nifty complement to the hoses—to subdue black demonstrators?

Hose down a bunch of kids? Hilton thought. *When the majority were protesting peacefully? What year are we living in?*

As soon as the game was officially postponed that Monday, Hilton left Camden Yards and headed to the epicenter of the trouble on North Avenue. There, he says, he spent hours—along with dozens of other African American men, young and old—urging calm and pleading with demonstrators to go home.

But when the Orioles announced that today's game would be held behind locked gates with no fans, Hilton felt compelled to return to the ballpark. Something in his soul told him he needed to experience this unprecedented day in baseball history firsthand, and to report on it as extensively as he could for the followers of his website.

So he showed up this morning at the media entrance with his expired credential from two days ago, hoping he might bluff his way in. But there was no need for that. The bored-looking security guard on duty simply waved him through, apparently under the impression that only accredited reporters or the seriously deranged would brave the turmoil in the streets to mingle with sweaty, harried men and women on deadline.

For nine innings Hilton watched the game quietly from a back row of the press box, awed to find himself in the company of such luminaries as ESPN's Tim Kurkjian and the *Baltimore Sun*'s Peter Schmuck, both of whom he'd read and seen on TV for years.

Now Hilton has made his way to this packed postgame presser, leaning against a back wall and nervously awaiting the appearance of the Orioles' manager.

To say he stands out in this room full of mostly middle-aged reporters is an understatement. In the first place the only other African American is veteran *Sun* videographer Kevin Richardson.

Then there is the matter of Hilton's attire.

When he showed up for Monday's game he'd looked every bit the young professional in a pressed polo shirt, khakis, and dress shoes polished to a high shine.

Today's outfit, however, is decidedly more casual: ball cap worn backward, T-shirt with a picture of Adam Jones holding a WWE championship belt, cargo shorts, Nike kicks, a backpack that looks roomy enough for a trek through the Himalayas.

The Nikes are the Kyrie Irving Easter edition, too, electric pink of a brightness that could sear one's retinas if stared at for too long.

And Hilton is definitely drawing stares, especially from the more buttoned-down TV reporters with their pricey haircuts and bespoke suits. As he inches his way to the front of the room they eye him like he's a fly that just landed in their salad.

But Hilton doesn't care. He didn't dress today to blend in. He dressed today to deliver a message.

This is me. This is who I am, his look says. *Just like the young brothers out there on the streets calling for change.*

As soon as Showalter settles in behind the microphone he spots Hilton. Over the years Showalter has made a habit of studying the audience at his press conferences, gazing nervously from side to side before he speaks.

"My eyes flit everywhere, to avoid problems before they happen," he once told author Pat Jordan for a lengthy sportsonearth.com profile.

Maybe this has something to do with being unceremoniously dumped by three different organizations throughout his stellar Major League career, three woeful teams he resuscitated only to be told a few years later: "Thanks, we'll take it from here."

Maybe it's just his innate wariness. Or maybe it's something deeper, something about control or an innate fight-or-flight response. Something you'd need a battery of shrinks and years of analysis to ferret out.

Whatever the reason, he's especially cautious in situations like this: a room full of dozens of national reporters he's never seen before, many in town to cover the unrest but now pressed into service to report on this weird-ass ballgame, too.

In this case, though, it takes no great powers of observation to see that the skinny black dude with the goatee and rapper vibe is out of his element. But Showalter feels some sort of reckoning coming with this young man too.

Something about Hilton's body language gives it away, the way he leans forward on his toes, practically quivering with anticipation as the press conference begins.

He's got something on his mind, Showalter thinks. *There's no doubt about it.*

As is customary, the presser kicks off with a few softball questions lobbed at the Orioles' manager:

"What was it like being in that atmosphere today?"

"How proud are you of Ubaldo's performance?"

"Could you really hear the bullpen phone ringing from the dugout?"

Hilton, who has now made his way to Showalter's immediate left, listens with growing impatience.

Uh-uh, he thinks. *This isn't gonna cut it. We're in this stadium with no fans because of what's going on outside, not inside. The game isn't the focus. Don't we have bigger things to talk about here?*

Up to this point he really hasn't formulated a question for Showalter. But he fears he might get shut out if he's silent for much longer. He also worries that no one else wants to bring up the not-insignificant matter of a civic rebellion that took place less than two days ago in and around his old neighborhood.

So Kendall Hilton decides to wing it.

This is history, he tells himself. *This is a moment we're going to be talking about a hundred years from now. So take full advantage of it.*

During the next lull in the back-and-forth, he finally speaks up. All eyes cut to him the moment he opens his mouth.

His question is direct, non-baseball in nature, and freighted with social significance. Which means it's the kind of question that would make your average Major League manager blanch and reach for the Pepto-Bismol.

"Buck," Hilton says, "I'm a resident from here. I grew up in, like, the neighborhoods [where] everything is happening. What advice would you give to the young black males in the city? Because you're well-respected in that area."

Whether a fifty-eight-year-old Southern white guy in a sport with an ever-diminishing African American fan base is truly held in high regard by the citizens of West Baltimore is debatable.

Watching the televised presser at home, Showalter's wife, Angela, reacts with a start.

Wow, she thinks, *that's a scary question to ask. It's one that you can be penalized for, maybe for the rest of your life . . .*

She mouths a silent prayer: *Don't blow it, Buck.*

Still, although the ever-cooperative Showalter is clearly blind-sided by the query, he doesn't shy away from it.

Gamely, he attempts an answer.

After a couple of false starts—a thought that trails off here, an analogy that peters out there—he seems to find some shaky footing.

"You know, I've never been black, okay?" he says. "So I don't know. You know, I can't put myself there. I've never been, you know, faced the challenges that they face, okay? So I understand the emotion, but I don't, you know, I can't . . . it's a pet peeve of mine when somebody says, 'Well, you know, I know what they're feeling. Why don't they do this? Why [doesn't] somebody do that?' You have never been black, okay? So just slow down a little bit.

"But you know, I try not to get involved in something that I don't know about. But I do know that it's something that is very passionate. Something that I am, with my upbringing, that it bothers me and it bothers everybody else. But you know, I just, can we . . . I understand we've made quite a statement as a city, some good, some bad. But now let's get on with taking the statement we've made and creating a positive.

"I want to be a . . . we talk to players . . . I want to be a rallying force for our city, you know? And [that] doesn't mean necessarily playing good baseball.

"You know, it just means, you know, everything we can do to—there are some things I don't want to be normal, you know what I mean? I don't. I want us to learn from some stuff that's going on, on both sides of it. And none of us—you know, I could talk about it for hours. But, you know, that's how I feel about it."

It is not, by any measure, a terribly eloquent answer.

It's not deep. Some would say it's not particularly thoughtful.

While Angela Showalter back home breathes a sigh of relief that her husband has not self-immolated and blurted out something impolitic that will dog him forever, Buck knows he has stumbled a bit—although not from a lack of effort.

With a few more minutes to think about it, he knows he could have come up with something more contemplative and nuanced.

Something about seeing so much discrimination growing up in a small town in the segregated Deep South. Something about seeing so many of the black players he's managed over the years work so hard to escape their own impoverished neighborhoods.

Something about how far we've come as a society when it comes to social justice—and how far we've yet to go.

The thought of this lost moment causes a momentary pang of anguish in the veteran skipper.

Wouldn't it be great if we could talk about this openly and purely and talk about exactly what you're thinking and feeling? he thinks. *Wouldn't it be great to sit here and talk about why everybody is mad or not mad? If everyone could really express themselves without worrying about the repercussions? How much better off we'd be!*

(Yet when Showalter's comments are relayed later to Adam Jones, the center fielder's first thought is: *He nailed it. That's the perfect answer. He doesn't KNOW. For him to say, "Well, y'all need to stop shooting each other, y'all need to get out and get jobs," that's one of the dumbest answers you can give.*)

In the seconds after Hilton's question and Showalter's halting answer, an uncomfortable silence descends upon the room.

The Orioles' PR people look stricken. Kristen Hudak, the team's new PR director, groans inwardly.

"That's it, I'm gonna be fired," she's overheard whispering.

Not only has someone without a valid credential managed to invade the sanctity of the postgame presser, the interloper even managed to bushwhack the Orioles' manager with a tough, politically tinged question.

A question that touched on the third rail of race, no less!

Yet Kendall Hilton, like Adam Jones, is thrilled with Showalter's response. No, he is *beyond* thrilled. He's nearly giddy as he replays the exchange in his mind.

"He gave me this look like he was really paying attention," Hilton will say later. "He looked at my face the whole time. Once he said, 'I'm not black,' I thought, 'This is it!' It's one thing to see those kinds of honest moments, those kinds of candid interviews on TV.

"But to actually be in there and be a part of it . . . wow."

What Hilton appreciates most is that Showalter's words square with the central message the young man has conveyed to his white friends since Freddie Gray's death: your life is not my life. And you need to understand that.

"The whole Freddie Gray situation and the riots, people think this all happened overnight," he tells people. "No, this has been going on since I've been alive. People where I live don't trust the police. With my white friends, I have to tell them: the way you're raised to look at the police is completely different from how I was raised.

"I did not trust them. It's sad to say it like that, but it's the truth. They're not there in my community to protect and serve. They're there to enforce. Sometimes they take that power and they do the wrong things with it.

"This whole Freddie Gray situation, it was just the pot boiling over. People are tired of it."

The fact that Showalter, at least on an intuitive level, seemed to sense the difference between life in black America and life in white America buoys Hilton's spirits. The fact that the Orioles' manager listened to him respectfully and gave him an answer from the heart has left him totally adrenalized.

Damn! he thinks. *That was a great moment for me!*

The great moment, however, is about to come to an abrupt end.

Even as Showalter continues answering questions, Hilton sees the Orioles' media relations manager, Jim Misudek, making a beeline toward him.

In the best of circumstances, Misudek has the same sunny disposition as a tax collector. Now, in this role as the PR staff's heavy, he appears even more dour than usual.

When he reaches Hilton, Misudek does not mince words.

"You have to go," he says quietly.

Hilton nods.

"I understand," he says.

Yet even as he's banished he can feel his spirits soar as he heads for the elevator. Once inside he waits for the doors to close, presses the up button and lets out a scream.

It's a cry of pure joy, raw and fierce and cathartic, so loud he wishes they could hear it all the way up at Penn North.

26

IN THE IMMEDIATE AFTERMATH of this incredible extravaganza at Camden Yards, the rush is on to dissect it and issue a postmortem.

Those still here feel the need to put it in some sort of context—if not for future generations of baseball scholars who will surely study it, then for the average Joe or Jane who can't imagine what it was like to experience something like this strange affair in person.

"It's weird," longtime White Sox TV play-by-play analyst Ken "Hawk" Harrelson tells his viewing audience, "but not as weird as I thought it might be with no fans."

This seems like a rather mild take for the seventy-three-year-old Harrelson, the former All-Star first baseman and outfielder for four different teams who's been broadcasting Sox games for three decades and is still a genuine character.

That he's still wild and crazy, in fact, has just been confirmed by a fawning profile of the Hawk in *Rolling Stone* last week.

It recounts an incident from a few years back when an enraged Harrelson, after seeing Sox catcher A. J. Pierzynski beaned by a Texas Rangers' pitcher with no retaliation from his teammates, appeared outside the Rangers' clubhouse after the game, ready to personally whip the offending pitcher's ass. That the pitcher was nearly forty years younger and would undoubtedly have been the ass-whipper rather than the ass-whippee in a fistfight with a septuagenarian appeared not to have dawned on Harrelson.

Which, right there, say longtime Hawk watchers, shows you what a character he is.

Or maybe that he has a screw loose somewhere.

In any event, many find it surprising that such a free spirit is now so blasé about a baseball game bleached of its vibrancy by the empty stands.

On the other hand, for someone like Joe Angel, the long-time radio "Voice of the Orioles" for 105.7 The Fan, the game's weirdness quotient is off the charts.

The genial Angel has broadcast big-league baseball for thirty-nine years and is in his sixteenth year of calling Orioles games.

He prepared for this broadcast thinking the radio audience might be one of the largest the station has ever had. Why *wouldn't* Orioles fans, he reasoned, tune in in record numbers to listen to this historic event in their cars, or at work, or wherever they couldn't watch it on TV?

"To me, the audience had to be huge!" he says. "It's only an audience you could imagine. 'Cause you couldn't *see* them in front of you. And for me, that was the weirdest thing. If you're a broadcaster and you're broadcasting a Major League Baseball game, you feed on the crowd.

"That's what gets you going. That's what lights the match! The crowd! At the ballpark! That's what gives it pizzazz! You feel like the people who are in front of you, the people you're listening to and hearing on the broadcast, are the people out there listening that you can't see.

"So to me, it was so strange broadcasting like that when there was no crowd reaction."

As to whether the game achieved the "purity" that Adam Eaton and Buck Showalter and others seemed to long for is also up for debate. But it certainly was far different from anything they'd been through.

With big-league ball now so corporate and commercialized, baseball lifers of a certain age—such as Showalter—can be forgiven for feeling the game itself often gets lost in all the theatrics of the typical "ballpark experience."

For many, this desperate attempt by MLB to retain its current fan base and attract new and younger paying customers makes for a sensory overload that can be daunting.

Music blares continuously at today's games. Scoreboards the size of Imax screens flash nonstop video messages, advertisements, quizzes, fan contests, birthday shout-outs, and pleas to clap, cheer, even "GET ON YOUR FEET!"

There are playgrounds for kids and fish tanks where they can get up close and personal with sea creatures. Postgame fireworks and rock concerts are ubiquitous.

Forget munching on hotdogs, peanuts, and Cracker Jack—now you can order sushi burritos, chicken shawarma nachos, and lobster poutine. There's gourmet ice cream and tiramisu for dessert. And you can wash it all down with craft or imported beers from all over the planet, top quality wines, and artisanal cocktails.

"It's more like a trip to Disneyland than a ballgame," notes Lee Igel, a professor of sports management at New York University who's been following this fanless game with interest.

Actually, says Igel, expanding on his theme park analogy, the No-Fans Game felt "like the movie *National Lampoon's Vacation.* The Griswolds get to Walley World and it's closed! There's no music as they're walking through. There's no hum of other people. There's no sound of all the rides.

"And they went on with it, their day at the place! They did it anyway!" Just as the Orioles and White Sox pressed on with their dreary contest.

Still, it's this very "Disney-fication" of baseball that Showalter and so many other baseball men of his generation view with suspicion—if not outright hostility.

"Have we made the game better with all these bells and whistles?" the Orioles' manager often asks. "I call it noise pollution."

Throw in the fact that half the fans at a typical game seem to be either talking on their cell phones or staring down at them and it's fair to ask why they bothered to show up in the first place.

In his darker moments, though, Showalter wonders if his cranky musings make him some kind of baseball Cro-Magnon man, someone so out of step with today's fans that it's pathetic.

Do people like the game the way I do? he often asks himself. *Maybe they don't. It's not just the baseball for them. They have to be entertained in another way.*

Yet a game without fans, the very folks targeted by all the ballpark frills, is a listless, dreary affair, as Showalter, the rest of the Orioles, and the White Sox have now discovered.

Maybe there was a refreshing "throwback" quality to the Flomaton High Hurricanes vs. the Century High Blackcats in a stifling closed gym all those years ago. But at the Major League level, a baseball game without the roar of the crowd becomes practically narcoleptic.

Certainly, for observers like Gary Thorne and Jim Palmer, it seems to blow holes in the great Bill Russell's theory that someday big-time sports will be played inside giant TV studios, with only a few bored, gum-snapping cameramen and technicians looking on.

Many of the sportswriters who have just returned from Showalter's postgame presser are left with a similar feeling of disconnect as they hunch over their laptops, trying to sum up the oddity of what has just transpired.

"It was a baseball game, that's all it was on the scorecard; just another lopsided baseball game in an April that's so far been full of them," writes Jonathan Bernhardt in his column for *Guardian US*. "Professional baseball without a crowd is an eerie, uncomfortable thing to watch, a half-measure, a strange compromise that adds nothing while robbing the sport of the very reason that it exists.

"That it happened at all," he continues, "is a testament

to the crisis this city—and country—finds itself in. May it never happen again."

Yet the *Sun*'s Peter Schmuck, who has covered baseball for twenty-five years in Baltimore and for eleven years before that in California, has a more positive outlook as he sits down to write, the afternoon shadows lengthening over Camden Yards.

Seemingly little has changed outside on the streets. Soldiers still patrol, emergency sirens still pierce the air, and angry demonstrators are promising more angry demonstrations. All of Baltimore seems to be holding its collective breath, as if wondering if it can be pulled back from the scary precipice on which it finds itself.

Yet in the middle of all this Schmuck nevertheless sees something affirming in the curious nine-inning spectacle he has just witnessed.

"The baseball game wasn't important because it was a baseball game," he writes. "It was important because it was also a sign that life has to go on. Those who have been critical of the Orioles for playing at all don't get that, but those of us who were there when a terrible earthquake rocked the San Francisco Bay Area during the 1989 World Series have seen that there is some healing power in our national pastime.

"No kids' game is going to solve the deep-rooted problems that plague our society," he continues, "but sports do have the ability to bind a community together and, if nothing else, give a troubled town a chance to feel good about itself for one very strange afternoon."

27

IF THE GOOD PEOPLE of Baltimore weren't saddened and appalled enough over the rioting that had earned them such national and international notoriety, they were soon subjected to even more humiliation courtesy of *Saturday Night Live*.

Never one to shy away from controversy, the venerable NBC sketch-comedy show skewered the No-Fans Game the following weekend in a skit that depicted it as slightly wacky and tedious and portrayed the city as a dangerous hellhole.

With cast members Taran Killam and Kenan Thompson playing Orioles announcers Jim Palmer and Frank Robinson, the Hall of Fame slugger and another mythic figure from the team's past, the four-minute parody was rife with wink-wink racial double entendres and lame riot-related puns.

Typical of the strained grab for laughs was this opening exchange between "Robinson" and "Palmer" as they set the scene for viewers:

"Robinson": "The White Sox are coming in with two wins in a row, and Baltimore has just been on *fire* this week. (Pause. Embarrassed look.) Sorry for how I said that . . ."

"Palmer": "I agree with you, Frank. Compare the Orioles now to their series against the Blue Jays—Baltimore took an absolute *beating* from the boys in blue. (Appears to catch himself, followed by horrified look.) Don't know why I called them that. Do *not* know why. No one has ever called them that . . ."

The awkward skit dragged on and on, pulling over and over at the scab of Baltimore's wounded self-image.

Bobby Moynihan played a pitiable hot dog vendor wandering aimlessly through a vast sea of empty green seats, looking for customers.

The popular scoreboard game "Guess the Attendance" flashed these choices:

a) 45,202
b) 44,620
c) 31, including the players.

And the fan favorite "Kiss Cam" segment, in lieu of zeroing in on real spectators, showed Moynihan as the lonely hot dog vendor happily bussing one of his franks before two cops in riot helmets and tactical gear also smooched.

"Kiss Cam, sponsored by Kingsford charcoal," the Robinson character added. "Throw a brick, start a fire." Then, supposedly realizing his faux pas, he barked at an offscreen producer: "Is *anybody* screening this copy? Or are you just handing it to us sight unseen?"

Even in an unpretentious town with a charming ability to laugh at itself the jokes landed with a thud.

Certainly Baltimore was used to taking shots of all sorts from its many critics. But when those shots landed with all the nuance of sledgehammer blows in the wake of such a devastating week for the city, they seemed to hurt even more.

(That also had appeared to be the case months earlier when Stephen Colbert on Comedy Central had launched into a riff on global warming and climate change, declaring that if the problems weren't addressed "the entire country would become an uninhabitable wasteland—not just Baltimore." As if the gibe needed even more explanation, the show's producers had helpfully added a photo of abandoned and boarded-up rowhouses in the upper-left corner of the screen.)

Especially brutal in the SNL skit was the concluding scene, when show host Scarlett Johansson, playing sideline reporter "Amber Theoharris," was shown doing a final stand-up alongside a set of train tracks.

"Where are you, Amber?" "Palmer" asked her from up in the booth.

"I'm at the Baltimore Amtrak station," "Theoharris" replied. "I'm going to Newark, where I'll be safer."

"Hold that train! I'm coming, too!" "Robinson" shouted.

At which point the two announcers, upping the hokey quotient exponentially, pretended to rip off their headsets and bolt to join her on this metaphorical Last Chopper Out of Saigon.

If there was an ameliorating factor in all this mockery it was that the much-anticipated "Fight of the Century" between Floyd Mayweather and Manny Pacquiao was also broadcast that night.

The fight, which started around the same time as SNL, ended up going the distance—12 rounds—before Mayweather was declared the winner by unanimous decision. Theoretically it also ended up siphoning off many viewers—at least male viewers—who would normally have tuned in to SNL and seen Baltimore take another figurative gut punch.

Nevertheless, to a city already depicted as pathologically dangerous before the rioting it felt like the very worst case of piling on from a network show.

The skit would be mentioned prominently in the next day's *Sun* and *Washington Post*, as well as in local and national TV newscasts and websites. And it would be talked about with a mixture of resignation and gallows humor in Baltimore for many weeks.

Yet following the No-Fans Game, as the days went by and the Freddie Gray protests remained peaceful, the dominant emotion felt by Baltimoreans was a quiet hopefulness that calm would prevail.

No one pretended that the city's attendant ills—poverty, crime, drugs, racial divisions, failing schools, lack of jobs— would magically disappear anytime soon. But it was clear they could no longer be ignored.

Baltimore had much to be proud of: topflight universities, appealing architecture, a thriving art and music scene, innovative restaurants, a growing tech industry, a booming waterfront area, and a friendly, small-town feel and affordability unmatched by most other urban areas on the East Coast.

But the unrest had given voice to the citizens of its most distressed neighborhoods, and their cries for social justice could no longer be ignored.

Epilogue

THE FALLOUT FROM THE Freddie Gray unrest would be swift and unrelenting. In many cases it would disrupt lives, destroy careers, generate lurid national headlines, and keep the city on edge for months.

Two days after the No-Fans Game, Baltimore City State's Attorney Marilyn Mosby announced criminal charges against the six police officers involved in the arrest and transport of Gray.

The thirty-five-year-old Mosby, who had been on the job a little over three months, seemed nervous at first as she delivered her remarks before a ring of TV cameras and a small group of onlookers on the steps of the War Memorial in downtown Baltimore.

Gradually, though, she seemed to find her rhythm and her voice took on a soaring tone of righteous conviction.

Gray, she said, had been "illegally detained" by police after they made eye contact with him on April 12. Officers had not properly fastened him in a seat belt in the back of the police transport van in accordance with Baltimore Police Department general orders. They hadn't provided him with timely medical attention when he requested it, and when the van finally arrived at the Western District police station he was in cardiac arrest.

The medical examiner's office, she said, had ruled Gray's death a homicide. It was her job to move forward with the case. Cheers and cries of, "Yes!" and, "Thank you!" rang out from some in the crowd.

Toward the end of her eighteen-minute address Mosby added this, in a voice brimming with emotion:

"To the people of Baltimore and the demonstrators across America: I heard your call for 'no justice, no peace.' Your peace is sincerely needed as I work to deliver justice on behalf of this young man."

Even as she took pains to note that the charges were not an indictment of the entire police department, her announcement touched off jubilant horn-honking and sign-waving street celebrations in parts of the city. And it surely helped ensure that a fresh spate of rioting wouldn't break out anytime soon.

In the second week of July, amidst an alarming spike in violent crime following the unrest, Baltimore mayor Stephanie Rawlings-Blake fired police commissioner Anthony Batts.

At a news conference at City Hall, the mayor said Batts had become a "distraction" in the effort to lower the city's soaring homicide total, which stood at 155. This was fifty more than at the same period a year earlier.

But the ousting of Batts, an African American, also came on the heels of a police union report ripping the BPD leadership for its response to the unrest, saying its "passive stance" toward violent demonstrators had endangered rank-and-file members and citizens alike.

The mayor tapped Kevin Davis, the white deputy police commissioner and a veteran law enforcement official in the state, to be the interim commissioner.

In the first week of September the city reached a controversial $6.4 million civil settlement with the family of Freddie Gray. Just days later, the embattled mayor issued another bombshell announcement: she would not seek re-election.

Only forty-five years old and considered a rising star in Democratic Party politics, Rawlings-Blake had been criticized for months over her handling of the rioting. Over and over she had been portrayed as a remote and feckless leader who shrank in her role just when the city needed her most.

Now, she said, she needed to focus on getting Baltimore back on its feet rather than running for office.

"The last thing I want," she told reporters, "is for every

one of the decisions I make moving forward—at a time when the city needs me the most—to be questioned in the context of a political campaign."

In early December, William Porter was the first of the six police officers to go on trial in connection with Gray's death. He was charged with involuntary manslaughter, second-degree assault, reckless endangerment, and misconduct in office. Like all of the other officers he pleaded not guilty.

Twelve days later his case was declared a mistrial when the jury failed to reach a unanimous verdict, a development that would delay all the remaining trials. Although the city was tense and the verdict stunned and enraged many, only two arrests were made and an uneasy calm prevailed as community leaders and ordinary citizens alike called for peace.

"As night fell over the intersection of Pennsylvania and North avenues—the center of the riots that shook the city in April—a line of people a block long linked arms to urge against a repeat" of the rioting, the *Baltimore Sun* reported.

"'One city! One purpose!' they chanted and, 'Whose city? Our city!'"

In July 2016, after circuit court judge Barry G. Williams presided over three bench trials and acquitted three other police officers charged in Gray's death, prosecutors dropped all charges against the three remaining officers, including William Porter.

Thus ended perhaps the most sensational series of criminal cases in the modern history of Baltimore. Mosby, the ambitious young prosecutor, defended her initial decision to charge the officers with various offenses.

But the fact there were zero convictions throughout the expensive trials—the city estimated total costs at a whopping $7.4 million—represented a huge embarrassment for Mosby and her office.

It also seemed to greatly heighten the mistrust between her office and the police department, an ironic twist for a prosecutor with a long line of cops in her family background. (None of the six officers would go on to face internal departmental charges either.)

Almost a year after it was looted and burned, becoming a lasting image of a city spiraling out of control, the CVS Pharmacy in Penn North reopened.

After having been demolished and rebuilt, the store, in a tidy and modern-looking red-brick building, was back in business just in time for Easter. It proved to be a welcome shot in the arm for the neglected neighborhood, still reeling from the aftereffects of the unrest and worried for months that the company would abandon it for good.

In May 2016 the Baltimore Police Department unveiled new transport vans with TV cameras to help monitor driver and prisoner activity. A new use-of-force policy, as well as one for summoning medical help for prisoners, was soon implemented as well.

In August 2016, after an investigation triggered by Freddie Gray's death and initiated by the city, a U.S. Department of Justice report accused the BPD of making unlawful stops, searches, and arrests of African Americans and of using excessive force.

"This pattern or practice is driven by systemic deficiencies in BPD's policies, training, supervision, and accountability structures that fail to equip officers with the tools they need to police effectively and within the bounds of the federal law," the highly critical report concluded.

In January 2017 Baltimore and the Justice Department entered into a consent decree that mandated major police reforms and federal monitoring of the city to ensure compliance.

As for the two teams that played in baseball's strangest game ever, both struggled to play consistently throughout the rest of the season.

After their general manager, Rick Hahn, had given the

team a failing grade the year before for not winning a title, the White Sox, despite some big-name signings, finished fourth in the American League Central with a 76-86 record.

The Orioles managed to win two of three games in their "home" series against Tampa Bay immediately following the No-Fans Game. But after having won their first division title in seventeen years in 2014, they finished a disappointing 81-81, sliding to third place in the AL East.

While their TV ratings remained strong, the Orioles also labored to fill seats at Camden Yards following the April unrest. Not helping matters was the city's alarming homicide rate. The total spiked dramatically to 344, making it Baltimore's second-deadliest year ever, eclipsed only by the 353 homicides recorded in 1993.

With the majority of season-ticket sales finalized before the start of the season, the Orioles' attendance drop in 2015 was not terribly alarming. It fell from a total of 2.4 million fans to 2.2 million.

But attendance would drop by nearly 10 percent in 2016, when the Orioles bounced back to finish 89-73 and lose the AL wild card game to the Toronto Blue Jays. (According to the *Sun*, it was the fifth-largest attendance drop in Major League Baseball.) And it would drop more than 6 percent in 2017, when they finished last in the division.

Team officials were reluctant to trace the issue directly back to the Freddie Gray riots. Yet with many downtown hotels, restaurants, bars, museums, and other attractions reporting significant declines in foot traffic and revenue since the unrest, it was hard not to conclude that it had a lingering effect on the public's perception of Baltimore as unsafe.

In February 2018 *USA Today* named Baltimore the deadliest big city in the country.

As for Freddie Carlos Gray, the main protagonist in the tragic drama that began on that sunny April morning four years ago, his grave sits on a sloping rise near the entrance to Woodlawn Cemetery in the Baltimore suburbs.

The grave is marked by a rose-colored headstone affixed with a photo of Gray gazing serenely into the camera. Not far away is a giant spreading oak tree and a shimmering lake where geese gather at the water's edge.

Visitors come occasionally and leave flowers, tiny wooden crosses, and other tokens, although their numbers seem to dwindle with each passing year.

Appendix

Official Box Score
Wednesday, April 29, 2015
Orioles 8, White Sox 2

	1	2	3	4	5	6	7	8	9	R	H	E
CWS (8-10)	0	0	0	0	2	0	0	0	0	2	4	1
BAL (10-10)	6	0	1	0	1	0	0	0		8	11	1

Chi White Sox	AB	R	H	RBI	BB	SO	LOB	AVG
Eaton, CF	3	0	0	0	0	1	0	.192
Bonifacio, E, PH[a]	1	0	1	0	0	0	0	.077
Cabrera, Me, LF	4	0	1	0	0	0	1	.268
Abreu, 1B	4	0	0	0	0	2	2	.296
LaRoche, DH	3	1	0	0	1	2	1	.200
Garcia, A, RF	3	1	2	0	0	1	0	.292
Gillaspie, 3B	3	0	0	0	0	0	3	.191
Ramirez, A, SS	3	0	0	0	0	1	1	.194
Soto, C	3	0	0	1	0	1	1	.136
Johnson, M, 2B	3	0	0	0	0	1	1	.244
Totals	30	2	4	1	1	9	10	.236

a. Singled for Eaton in the 9th.

Baltimore	AB	R	H	RBI	BB	SO	LOB	AVG
De Aza, LF-RF	3	1	1	0	1	0	2	.233
Paredes, DH	4	1	0	0	0	2	3	.385
Young, D, RF	4	1	1	0	0	0	0	.357
Lough, LF	0	0	0	0	0	0	0	.300
Jones, A, CF	3	0	1	1	0	1	0	.400
Davis, C, 1B	4	1	1	3	0	2	1	.268
Machado, 3B	4	3	3	1	0	0	1	.254
Cabrera, E, SS	4	1	2	1	0	1	0	.250
Joseph, C, C	4	0	2	2	0	1	0	.327
Navarro, R, 2B	4	0	0	0	0	0	3	.250
Totals	34	8	11	8	1	7	10	.286

Batting

TB: Garcia, A 2; Bonifacio, E; Cabrera, Me.

RBI: Soto (2).

Runners left in scoring position, 2 out: Johnson, M; LaRoche.

GIDP: Gillaspie; Abreu.

Team RISP: 0-for-6.

Team LOB: 2.

Fielding

E: Abreu (2, throw).

DP: (Samardzija–Ramirez, A–Abreu).

Batting

2B: Machado (4, Samardzija); Cabrera, E 2 (2, Samardzija, Samardzija); Jones, A (6, Carroll).

HR: Davis, C (5, 1st inning off Samardzija, 2 on, 1 out); Machado (4, 5th inning off Samardzija, 0 on, 1 out).

TB: Davis, C 4; Joseph, C 2; Cabrera, E 4; Jones, A 2; Young, D; De Aza; Machado 7.

RBI: Jones, A (19); Davis, C 3 (16); Cabrera, E (4); Joseph, C 2 (6); Machado (12).

Runners left in scoring position, 2 out: Paredes; Machado.

SF: Jones, A.

GIDP: De Aza.

Team RISP: 5-for-10.

Team LOB: 4.

Fielding

E: Machado (5, throw).

DP: 2 (Navarro, R–Machado–Davis, C; Machado–Navarro, R–Davis, C).

Chi White Sox	IP	H	R	ER	BB	SO	HR	ERA
Samardzija (L, 1-2)	5.0	10	8	7	1	5	2	4.78
Carroll	2.0	1	0	0	0	1	0	0.00
Rodon	1.0	0	0	0	0	1	0	5.40
Totals	8.0	11	8	7	1	7	2	4.18

Baltimore	IP	H	R	ER	BB	SO	HR	ERA
Jimenez (W, 2-1)	7.0	3	2	0	1	6	0	1.59
Gausman	1.0	0	0	0	0	2	0	4.91
Britton	1.0	1	0	0	0	1	0	1.93
Totals	9.0	4	2	0	1	9	0	4.78

Game Scores: Samardzija 17; Jimenez 74.

Pitches-strikes: Samardzija 87-62; Carroll 20-15; Rodon 5-5; Jimenez 89-61; Gausman 15-11; Britton 11-7.

Groundouts-flyouts: Samardzija 4-4; Carroll 3-0; Rodon 1-1; Jimenez 9-3; Gausman 1-0; Britton 2-0.

Batters faced: Samardzija 26; Carroll 7; Rodon 3; Jimenez 24; Gausman 3; Britton 4.

Umpires: HP: Jerry Layne. 1B: Hunter Wendelstedt. 2B: Bob Davidson. 3B: David Rackley.

Weather: 73 degrees, sunny.

Wind: 4 mph, Out to LF.

First pitch: 2:06 PM.

T: 2:03.

Venue: Oriole Park at Camden Yards.

Sources

IN ORDER TO TELL the story of baseball's strangest game and the tumultuous setting in which it unfolded, I relied mostly on interviews with many of the main personalities and much research, as well as the knowledge of Baltimore and its baseball team informed by my thirty-two years as a columnist, sportswriter, and features writer for the *Baltimore Sun*.

For some of the background on the unrest I pored over the crackerjack reporting of my former colleagues at the *Sun*, as well as that done by the *Washington Post*, the *New York Times*, *USA Today*, the *Chicago Tribune*, and the Associated Press.

As we live in a world in which seemingly every event, large or small, is captured on camera, I also relied on video—mainly from YouTube, CNN, FOX News, and the four local network affiliates, WJZ-TV, WBAL-TV11, WMAR-TV, and WBFF-FOX 45—for information on the Saturday-night confrontation outside Camden Yards between demonstrators, bar patrons, and police; Freddie Gray's funeral at New Shiloh Baptist Church; the frightening spate of rioting that erupted in Baltimore the same day; the Tuesday-night confrontation between veteran newsman Geraldo Rivera and protesters; and the many news conferences held in the ensuing days by the mayor's office, police department spokespersons, attorneys and spokespersons for Freddie Gray, and representatives of the Baltimore City State's Attorney's Office.

Also of invaluable assistance in my research was the original broadcast of the Orioles–White Sox No-Fans Game on the Mid-Atlantic Sports Network (MASN), with lead announcer Gary Thorne and analyst Jim Palmer.

The National Baseball Hall of Fame and Museum in Cooperstown, New York, was critical in providing information about—and steering me to—the MLB Authentication Program.

The esteemed Society for American Baseball Research (SABR) was an important source for statistics and other minutiae regarding baseball's least-attended games. And *Street & Smith's Sports Business Journal* provided useful information on the Orioles' TV ratings, while *Forbes* did the same with figures concerning the Orioles' revenue and net worth.

Finally, the Orioles' website was indispensable in the course of this project, and information from the fine websites Bleacher Report and the defunct Sports on Earth helped lend nuance to what I hope is a dramatic and insightful chronicle of a singular baseball game that helped give a desperate city what it needed most: hope.

Index

Abreu, Jose, 79, 81, 86, 138

Alsop, Marin, 130

Anaheim Angels, 61

Angel, Joe, 151

Angelos, John, 15, 18, 19, 102–8, 118

Angelos, Margaret, 18, 104

Angelos, Peter, 15, 51–52, 62, 103, 105–6, 118–19

Antonen, Mel, 98–99

Antonen, Ray, 98–99

Bader, Greg, 15, 42, 81

Baldwin, Brooke, 114–15, 116

Baltimore MD: curfew in, 32–33, 43, 129–30; on edge, 34–45; efforts to calm citizens of, 129–31; financial settlement of, with Gray family, 160; history of segregation in, 68; homicide rate in, 160, 163; military and police presence in, 2, 4, 7, 11, 13, 24, 28, 32, 35–36, 46, 56–57, 64, 100–102, 117, 125; mocked on television, 154–57; nicknames for, 20; peace in, 19–20; social conditions in, 5–6, 9, 41, 44, 49, 68–69, 105, 115–16, 126, 157; violence and property damage in, 4–5, 12–17, 23–45, 92, 93, 115, 125–26

Baltimore Museum of Industry, 130

Baltimore Orioles: and attendance at 1972 game vs. White Sox, 60; before No-Fans Game, 52–55; Boston Red Sox and, 19, 134; and drops in attendance, 163; and game postponement and practice, 34–45; and remainder of 2015 season, 163; and Reviving Baseball in Inner Cities program, 69; St. Louis Browns and, 117–18; television ratings of, 62

Baltimore Orioles fans: and ball girls, 89; at Hilton Hotel, 94;

impact of absence of, 77–78, 81, 89, 113, 123–24; at left-field gates, 75, 82, 90–95, 114, 124–25; "Lost Generation" of, 90–91

Baltimore Police Department (BPD): accusations against, 6, 22, 66, 68, 107, 114–16; and news conference about Freddie Gray's death, 11; officers charged in Freddie Gray's death, 159–62; and protests and violence, 4, 13–18, 23–29, 33–46, 100–104, 125–26; and questions about Freddie Gray's death, 126–29; reforms to, 162

Baltimore Sun, 68, 69, 92, 94–95, 116, 126, 127, 157, 161, 163

Baltimore Symphony Orchestra, 130–31

baseball games, generally: and current "baseball experience," 151–53; Gary Thorne on importance of, 111–12; unusual events at, 59–61

Batts, Anthony, 11, 40, 160

BearCat (Ballistic Engineered Armored Response Counter Attack Truck), 25

Beckham, Gordon, 56, 132

Bernhardt, Jonathan, 99–100, 153–54

Bernstein, Leonard, 130

Berry, Quintin, 69

Black Guerilla Family, 21

Black Lives Matter movement, 10

Blitzer, Wolf, 25

Bloods, 21

Bonafacio, Emilio, 138

Boston Marathon bombings, 61

Boston Red Sox, 12–14, 17, 19, 61, 134

Bowie Baysox, 73

Bradley, Andrea, 69

Britton, Martha Rosamaria, 65

Britton, Zach, 52–53, 55, 64–66, 137–38

Brown, Michael, 10, 11, 12

Brubaker, Carol, 86

Bryant, Jamal, 18, 19, 22, 27

Bullock, Allen, 127

Burnett, Erin, 40

Cabrera, Everth, 82, 83, 112

Cabrera, Melky, 78–79, 138

Camden Yards, 6, 12–17, 19–20, 35–36, 46, 56–57, 154

Carroll, Scott, 83, 133

Carter, Willie, 50

CBS, 107, 134

Charleston Riverdogs, 59

Charm City Comedy Festival, 129

Chicago White Sox, 28–30, 52–55, 60, 79–80, 142, 162–63

Cincinnati Reds, 60

Clemente, Roberto, 61

CNN, 25, 40–41, 114–16

Colbert, Stephen, 156

Columbus (OH) Red Stixx, 59

Comedy Central, 156

Conaway, Vernon, Jr., 15

Cooper, Anderson, 40

Cooper, Don, 83

Crips, 21, 27

Cummings, Elijah E., 20

curfew, 32–33, 43, 129–30

CVS pharmacy, 26, 28, 37, 115, 162

Darden, Gloria, 23

Davidson, Bob, 84–86, 87, 88

Davidson, Denise, 86

Davis, Chris, 35, 65; Adam Jones and, 64–66; after No-Fans Game, 140–41; before No-Fans Game, 3, 53, 118; during No-Fans Game, 81–82, 112–13, 122, 124, 134; game postponements and, 30–34, 36; Jeff Samardzija and, 79–80

Davis, Jill, 33

Davis, Kevin, 160

De Aza, Alejandro, 80, 83

Democracy Now!, 107

Dempsey, Rick, 7

Denver, John, 55, 132–33

Diallo, Amadou, mother of, 21

Dorin, Paul, 94

Dubroff, Rich, 100–102

Dubroff, Susan, 101

Duquette, Amy, 47

Duquette, Dan, 47, 91

Eaton, Adam, 28, 53–55, 77–78, 80, 136, 139

Empowerment Temple AME Church, 18, 43

Encina, Eduardo, 95, 118

Essian, Jim, 97

Fan-I Sports, 141–42

fans. *See* Baltimore Orioles fans

"Fight of the Century," 156–57

Finley, Charles O., 96

Florida Marlins, 60

FlowerMart, postponement of, 130

Frederick Douglass High School, 24, 125–26

Fugett, Jean, 69–70

Garcia, Avisail, 83, 112, 131

Garner, Eric, 10, 11, 21, 129

Gausman, Kevin, 134, 135, 136

Gibson, Bob, 61

Gillaspie, Conor, 112, 131

Goldberg, Whoopi, 40

Graham, Michael, 39–41, 42

Graham, Toya, 39–42

Gray, Freddie Carlos, 19, 92, 129; arrest, transport, and death of, 9–11; funeral and interment of, 20–23, 116; grave of, 163–64; Kendall Hilton on, 148–49; news conference about death of, 11; police officers charged in death of, 159–62; questions about death of, 126–29

Gray, Fredericka, 17–18, 19

Gray family, 10, 19, 21, 22, 27, 118, 160

Gregory, Dick, 21
Guardian US, 99, 153

Hahn, Rick, 162–63
Hannity, Sean, 44–45
Harrelson, Ken "Hawk," 150–51
Heard, Jehosie "Jay," 117–18
Heaverlo, Dave, 96
Hilton, Kendall, 141–42, 143–49
Hilton Hotel, 94
Hogan, Larry, 11, 32, 37, 127–28
Hollander, Brett, 103–4
Holmes, Larry, 12
Holt, Lester, 116
Hudak, Kristen, 16, 148
Hunter, Jim, 58
Hunter, Tommy, 30–31, 33–34, 35, 36, 141
Hurricane Irene, 60
Hutcheson, Brad, 93

Igel, Lee, 152

Jackson, Jesse, 20, 22, 107
Jacobson, Mark, 95–98
Jett, Joan, 110–11
Jimenez, Ubaldo, 73–75, 77–79, 112, 131–32, 138
Johansson, Scarlett, 156
Johnson, Micah, 83, 112
Jones, Adam LaMarque: background and family of, 68–70; on Buck Showalter's comments, 148; during No-Fans Game, 81, 86–87, 124–25, 133; experiences of, as black man, 66–67; game postponements and, 31; remarks of, before No-Fans Game, 63–64, 70–72, 76, 118; on rioters' motivations, 30, 66, 67–68; on violence, 14
Jones, Audie, 1, 3
Jordan, Pat, 51, 144
Joseph, Brooke, 31, 32
Joseph, Caleb: after No-Fans Game, 139; before No-Fans Game, 55, 56, 72–73, 74; during No-Fans Game,

78, 83, 87, 124; game postponements and, 31–32
Joseph P. Riley Jr. Park, 59

Kansas City Royals, 79–80
Kennedy, John F., 130
Key, Keegan-Michael, 38
Killam, Taran, 155
King, Martin Luther, Jr., 27, 61, 72, 76, 117
King, Rodney, 61, 85
Kubatko, Roch, 71
Kurkjian, Tim, 143

LaRoche, Adam, 112, 131, 138
Lasorda, Tommy, 84
Law Enforcement Officers Bill of Rights, 128
Layne, Jerry, 78, 87–88, 124
Letterman, David, 113
Lieberman, Rich, 96
Loma Prieta earthquake, 61, 99, 154
Los Angeles Dodgers, 61, 84, 85
Lough, David, 17

M&T Bank Stadium, 29, 36
Machado, Manny, 82, 83, 86, 112, 113–14, 122, 134
Major League Baseball Authentication Program, 121–24
Manfred, Rob, 29
Marshall, Thurgood, 126
Martin, Trayvon, sister of, 21
Mayweather, Floyd, 156–57
McCord, Gary, 134
media: and Adam Jones's remarks, 63–64, 70–72; and coverage of riots, 28, 37–38, 43–45; and Freddie Gray's death, 11; at No-Fans Game, 95–102; Toya Graham and, 40–41
memorabilia, authentication of, 120–24
Merguerian, Dawn, 95
Mfume, Kweisi (Frizzell Gray), 20–21, 38, 40–41, 114–19
Mid-Atlantic Sports Network (MASN), 32, 58, 62, 71, 75, 108–9, 138

Minnesota Twins, 98–99, 139

Misudek, Jim, 136, 149

Mondawmin Mall, 23–24, 28, 39, 41, 100, 125, 130, 142

Montreal Expos, 61, 84, 85

Moore, Wes, 107

Mosby, Marilyn, 127, 159–60, 161

Mosby, Nick, 119

Moynihan, Bobby, 155

Murphy, William "Billy," Jr., 10, 22, 107

Nader, Ralph, 103, 106

National Guard, 2, 4, 32, 35, 37, 56–57, 64, 101–2, 117, 125

Nation of Islam, 26–27

Navarro, Rey, 83

New York Times, 94

New York Yankees, 61, 113, 134

Nightly News (NBC), 116

No-Fans Game: and Caleb Joseph and pretend crowd, 72–73; costs and controversies of, 62–63; decision to play, 42–43; fans "attending," 75, 82, 90–95, 114, 124–25; final score of, 138; and impact of lack of fans, 77–78, 81, 89, 113, 123–24; by inning, 77–83, 87, 109, 112–14, 131–33, 135–38; "normalcy" for Baltimore and, 53, 68–70, 76, 118, 140; official box score of, 165–68; and police and military personnel, 56–57; and postgame emotions, 139–41; postgame reflections on, 150–54; and public mood in Baltimore, 125–26; and regular game events, 55–56; teams before, 52–55, 73–75; umpires and, 78, 84–90; as unusual, 46–48, 58, 61

Oakland Athletics, 61, 96–98, 110

Obama, Barack, 21, 32, 38, 71, 129

O'Day, Darren, 14

Olbermann, Keith, 103, 106

Operation Bullpen, 122

"Orioles Magic (Feel It Happen)," 139

Ortiz, David, 123

Orzol, Steve, 92

Pacquiao, Manny, 156–57

Paige, Edith, 50

Palmer, Jamie, 111

Palmer, Jim, 76, 80–81, 83, 108–12, 133–34, 136, 153

Palmer, Kelly, 111

Paredes, Jimmy, 81, 83, 109

Petroskey, Dale, 76

Pierzynski, A. J., 150

Pitro, Chris, 94

Pittsburgh Pirates, 139

police. *See* Baltimore Police Department (BPD)

The Police (band), 110–11

Porter, William, 161

Posner, Michael, 123

Powell, Boog, 6–7

Prann, Elizabeth, 14

Pugh, Catherine, 44–45

Rackley, David, 88

Ramirez, Alexei, 81, 86, 112, 135

Rawlings-Blake, Stephanie, 21, 92, 127, 128; and curfew announcement, 32–33; and lack of communication, 25–26; reaction of, to initial protests, 11, 17–18; replaces police commissioner, 160–61; "space to destroy" comment of, 37–38; "thug" comment of, 38, 128

Reinhard, Dennis, 15–17, 56–57

Revering, Dave, 97

Rice, Tamir, 10, 11

Richardson, Kevin, 143

Riehl, Chris, 95

Ripken, Cal, Jr., 43, 47–48, 91

Rivera, Geraldo, 44–45

Robinson, Jackie, 117

Rose, Kwame, 44

Runaways (band), 111

Russell, Bill, 135, 153

Rutherford, Rick, 121–25
Ryan, Nolan, 139–40

Sale, Chris, 80
Samardzija, Jeff, 3, 79–83, 87, 113–14
San Francisco Giants, 61
Sarbanes, John, 20
Saturday Night Live, 154–57
Sauers, Perry, 121–23
Savage, Bill, 61–62
Scharper, Julie, 19
Schmuck, Peter, 143, 154
Schoop, Jonathan, 82
Scott, Brandon, 129
Scott, Walter, 10, 11, 107
Seattle Mariners, 69, 96–98
Selig, Bud, 61
September 11 terrorist attacks, 61
Showalter, Angela, 146, 147
Showalter, Bill, 49–50
Showalter, Buck, 91, 113; April 25
    game and, 14, 17; background of,
    49–50; before No-Fans Game, 75;
    on current "baseball experience,"
    152–53; during No-Fans Game, 79,
    114; and game postponement, 30;
    home field advantage and, 134–35;
    pregame concerns of, 50–52; pre-
    game remarks of, 118; and previous
    fanless games, 48–49; questioned
    by Kendall Hilton, 141, 143–49
Showalter, Lina, 49–50
Society for American Baseball
    Research (SABR), 59–61
Soto, Geovany, 81, 112, 124, 135, 136
Spikes, Iona, 126
Sports Business Journal, 62
Sports Illustrated, 135
"Star-Spangled Banner," 55, 77, 91–
    92, 130–31
Stein, Ben, 40
Sting, 110–11
St. Louis Browns, 117–18
Stokes, Carl, 40–41
Strachan, Dolores, 101

"Take Me Out to the Ballgame," 132
Tampa Bay Devil Rays, 34, 42, 59,
    140–41, 163
Texas Rangers, 150
"Thank God I'm a Country Boy," 55,
    132–33
Thomas, Thurman, 106–7
Thompson, Kenan, 155
Thorne, Gary, 75–76, 78, 80–81, 82,
    108–9, 111–12, 132–36, 138, 153
Thornton, Gregory, 126
Toronto Blue Jays, 155, 163
Troy (NY) Trojans, 59
Twitter, 18, 54–55, 92, 102–8, 118

Uehara, Koji, 30
University of Maryland—
    Baltimore, 24
USA Today, 94, 163

Valentine, Bobby, 97
Veeck, Bill, 59
Veeck, Mike, 59–60
Ventura, Robin, 28, 75, 86, 139–40
Vice Sports, 96

Wagner, Ryan, 77
Waldman, Suzyn, 134
Wales (rapper), 126
Washington Post, 94, 157
Weaver, Earl, 91
Wendelstedt, Harry, 88, 89–90
Wendelstedt, Hunter, 87–90
Wieters, Matt, 31
Williams, Barry G., 161
Winfrey, Oprah, 40
WMAR-TV, 39, 42, 169
Worcester Ruby Legs, 59
World Series, 61, 99, 139, 154
WPWR, 62
Wright, Anson, 4

Yankee Stadium, 61
Young, Bernard C. "Jack," 19, 27, 119
Young, Delmon, 55, 81, 82, 133
Youppi! (Expos mascot), 84